Kynan Bridges is one of my favorite Bible teachers. We are on the precipice of the greatest revival and move of miracles in history. This book will prepare you to enter the last act of the last play!

SID ROTH,
Host, *It's Supernatural*

Kynan Bridges stirs up passion and hunger within the heart of the believer to long for and see the glory of God! In his latest book, *School of the Presence*, Kynan prepares the body of Christ to get ready to see this all-powerful God work in our lives and manifest His glory and kingdom.

DR. JEREMY LOPEZ
CEO, Identitynetwork.net

SCHOOL

of the

PRESENCE

OTHER BOOKS BY KYNAN BRIDGES

The Healing Handbook

Possessing Your Healing

90 Days to Possessing Your Healing

Power of Unlimited Faith

Supernatural Favor

SCHOOL

of the

PRESENCE

Walking in
POWER, INTIMACY, AND AUTHORITY
ON EARTH AS IT IS IN HEAVEN

KYNAN BRIDGES

DESTINY IMAGE® PUBLISHERS, INC.
P.O. Box 310, Shippensburg, PA 17257-0310
"Promoting Inspired Lives."

This book and all other Destiny Image and Destiny Image Fiction books are available at Christian bookstores and distributors worldwide.

Cover design by Eileen Rockwell
Interior design by Terry Clifton

For more information on foreign distributors, call 717-532-3040.
Reach us on the Internet: www.destinyimage.com.

ISBN 13 TP: 978-0-7684-1500-1
ISBN 13 eBook: 978-0-7684-1501-8
ISBN 13 HC: 978-0-7684-1624-4
ISBN 13 LP: 978-0-7684-1625-1

For Worldwide Distribution, Printed in the U.S.A.
1 2 3 4 5 6 7 8 / 21 20 19 18 17

I dedicate this book to the Lord Jesus Christ, the King of kings and Lord of lords. I also want to dedicate this book to my precious wife, Gloria Bridges—you are as beautiful as you are virtuous. You are the only mother of our 5 beautiful children (Ella, Naomi, Isaac, Israel, and Anna), and my number one supporter in life and ministry; I love you with all of my heart. To my church family (Grace & Peace Global Fellowship), who have been instrumental in praying for and supporting this project—God bless you!

ACNKOWLEDGMENTS

First of all, I want to take a moment and acknowledge my precious Lord and Savior Jesus Christ. It is through Him that I live, move, breathe, and possess the ability to write this and all books. To my wife, I honor and love you dearly. To my ministerial staff (especially my senior staff editor Crystal Dixon)—you are amazing! To my parents, James and Juanita Bridges— I honor you. To Destiny Image Publishers, thank you for believing in me and helping me to release this message to the Body of Christ. Special thanks to the production and editing team including: Larry Sparks, John Martin, and many others.

I also want to take a moment and acknowledge great men and women of the faith who have impacted my life in a positive way (either directly or indirectly) including: Pastor Wayne C. Thompson, Dr. Mark Chironna, Dr. Bill Hamon, Dr. James Goll, Dr. Heidi Baker, Pastor Bill Johnson, Sid Roth, Pastor Tony Kemp, Derek Prince, Smith Wigglesworth, John G. Lake, Oswald Chambers, John Wesley, Jack Coe, Oral Roberts, Kathryn Kuhlman, R. W. Shambach, Kenneth E. Wagin, Dr. T.L. Osborn, Archbishop Benson Idahosa, Dr. Martin Luther King, Jr., Mahesh Chavda, Hank and Brenda Kunneman, Apostle G. Maldonado, Apostle Charles Ndifon, Dr. Charles and Francis Hunter, Joan Hunter, Pastor Marlin Harris, Dr. E.V. Hill, Marilyn Hickey, Dr. T.L. Lowrey, Dr. Rodney Howard-Browne, Reinhard Bonnke, Dr. Douglas Wingate, and Benny Hinn. Thank you for your service and gift to the Body of Christ. God Bless you.

CONTENTS

INTRODUCTION

Years ago, I had a very profound experience that changed my life forever. I went to heaven! That's right, I went to heaven. It was one of the most surreal experiences I have ever had. From this experience, I reaffirmed my belief that heaven is a very real place and that the supernatural is a very real lifestyle for every believer.

The most memorable aspect of my visit to heaven was the reality of God's Presence. Jesus told me to tell the church that there is "so much more!" Since that time, I have been on an intentional mission to awaken God's people to the supernatural power of His presence. In fact, we can live in this powerful presence on a daily basis.

What if I told you that you can live a miraculous lifestyle no matter what your title or position in life? What if I told you that you could see the miracles of the Bible on a daily basis? Well, you can! This may very well be one of the most powerful and important books that I have ever written. As you read, I pray that you will open your heart to the Holy Spirit and allow Him to instruct and guide you through every page. I pray that you will receive a supernatural impartation of God's grace and anointing that will thrust you into a new dimension of the miraculous power of God. You can live in the consciousness of God's manifest presence every day of your life.

This book will give you the keys that you need to live the life you have dreamed of living. Today is your day! Read and release your faith for more.

CHAPTER 1

ON EARTH AS IT IS IN HEAVEN

I can vividly recall a supernatural experience that changed my life. Several years ago, I was traveling from England back to the United States. I had a great time teaching leaders how to operate in the supernatural. While on my flight back to the States, I closed my eyes and instantly I was in heaven. This did not seem like a dream or a vision at all; it was very real! In fact, it was so real that I assumed that my plane must have crashed.

I can remember thinking about my wife and children as if I would not see them again. My senses were heightened and suddenly awakened to the reality of eternity. It was so real I could literally feel the atmosphere; it was palpable. Every fiber of my being was aware that I was occupying another realm or dimension. Just moments later, I was back on the plane, back in the seat next to a lady who looked at me very strangely. Talk about in-flight entertainment!

While pondering what had just transpired, I saw the face of Jesus in front of me and I heard these words, "Tell My people there is so much more!" Then the face vanished away! This was probably one of the most profound experiences of my life. I was left with so many questions. What did He mean by that? What was the "more" He referred to? This heavenly encounter challenged me in ways that I cannot begin to describe. It literally rocked my world (as the expression goes). It was then that I realized that the average believer lives within the religious safety net of "church as usual" while simultaneously longing for a deeper experience with God.

Many are frustrated that what they read about in the Bible is not reflected in their mundane Christian lives. Countless others are disillusioned by the fact that the average Sunday service is not representing the powerful display of God's presence that is depicted in the Bible and exemplified by the early Church. We talk about miracles, signs, and wonders, and well-meaning authors and teachers even write about the supernatural. But what is missing from today's Church? The one key element, the element of which I was abundantly aware during my heavenly vision and the element many believers often neglect is the presence of God!

Without a single word being spoken to me, I knew I was in heaven because of God's overwhelming presence. Then it dawned on me—was this an isolated event, reserved for when we reach the "sweet by and by"? Is this only for those really great revivals that happen every so often? Or was it only for the super-spiritual or Christian celebrities? What if every believer could operate from this presence every single day?

After this experience, I began to teach a series on *Developing a Heavenly Vision*. In the pages of this book, I will divulge secrets that I learned from God Himself—the secrets that will unlock the power and authority that you have longed to operate in. You will come to discover that God's presence is not just for an occasional touch, but you and I can live from His presence on a daily basis. Miracles, signs, wonders, and deep intimacy with God can be a normal way of life. Do you want to live in the supernatural every day? Then this book is for you!

The presence of God is *not* an event or an experience; it is a lifestyle!

DEVELOPING A HEAVENLY VISION

I am reminded of one of my favorite verses in the Bible: *"Where there is no vision, the people perish"* (Prov. 29:18). Like me, you have probably heard this scripture referenced dozens of times. I have even heard it used at secular motivational seminars as a means of encouraging people to take charge of their lives by developing an actionable vision. But what if I told you that there were supernatural implications to this concept of vision? What if I told you that this scripture was not about self-motivation at all? What If I told you that this was one of the keys to unlocking a supernatural life? Before we can explore the powerful implications of possessing a heavenly vision, we must first understand what vision is.

Vision is vitally important in the life of the believer. You may be wondering what makes me say that. The New American Standard Bible's translation of Proverbs 29:18 is very explicit on the necessity of having a vision: *"Where there is no vision, the people are unrestrained"*

(NASB). To be *unrestrained* equals unchecked, unrepressed, and excessive. To put it simply, without vision a person is what many may describe as being "all over the place." This passage in Proverbs is much more than a word to the wise; it is just as much an exhortation as it is a warning. On the other hand, where there is vision, there is preparation, expectation, and manifestation.

When we picture what we want and determine what it will take, if it is truly a desire preparation *will* follow. And when we prepare, we have favorable expectations in mind of what the outcome will be. The word *vision* in Proverbs 29:18 comes from the Hebrew word *chazown*, which means "oracle, prophecy, or divine communication" (Strong's H2377). We can see that this is more than just a personal plan for one's life; this is an ecstatic, revelatory communication from God that transforms the way that we see, think, and imagine. When I experienced that supernatural vision on the plane that day, it literally transformed my life. I could never forget what I saw in the heavenly realm.

> If it does not transform your sight and change your life, it's not vision.

A sprinter doesn't *train* for months and even years to lose the race. Athletes don't *practice* months at a time to prepare for games and matches they don't assume will lead them to a championship. A family doesn't *plan* for the arrival of children they don't expect to have. Envisioning something and keeping that vision in front of you incites preparation and expectation for when it does happen. I can cite many more examples of how this principle applies in a natural sense, and I am sure you can do the same. If aspiring to achieve common, earthly prizes produces results, how much more, then, will having and developing a heavenly vision impact both our spiritual and natural lives?

While we occupy the earth, one of our mandates is to manifest the kingdom of heaven right here in this earthly realm, inviting God's will to be done here on earth "as it is in heaven." The word *developing* means to bring out the capabilities or possibilities of, to bring to a more advanced or effective state, to cause to grow or expand, and to bring into being or activity. What if I told you that you have the power, the ability, to manifest the culture of heaven in *every* area of your life? The Lord Jesus Christ has already given us this information.

In Matthew 16:19, the Lord told His disciples, *"And I will give unto thee the keys of the kingdom of heaven: and whatsoever thou shalt bind on earth shall be bound in heaven: and whatsoever thou shalt loose on earth shall be loosed in heaven."* The Message Bible puts it this way: *"And that's not all. You will have complete and free access to God's kingdom, keys to open any and every door: no more barriers between heaven and earth, earth and heaven. A yes on earth is yes in heaven. A no on earth is no in heaven."* Could the Scriptures be any clearer?

The Lord wants heaven and earth to be in perfect, harmonious agreement. This happens when we live our entire lives from the vantage point of heaven—from above. Live above issues. Live above struggles. Live above circumstances. Second Corinthians 5:7 sums it up well— live by faith in God, not by physical eyesight. When the Scripture talks about vision, it's talking about revelation.

The truth is, our lives can never transcend our level of revelation. What you see by revelation will determine the reality that you live in and from. This is why the Bible says that without a *heavenly vision* people perish. Millions of believers all over the world are perishing (casting off restraint and losing hope) because they do not possess a heavenly vision. They have no picture of the endless possibilities of God from heaven's perspective. They don't realize that God wants to use them to open the eyes of the blind, heal the sick, and raise the dead.

OPEN YOUR EYES

It is hard for some people to believe that we have spiritual senses that are just as important to us as our natural senses; in fact, they are even more important than our physical senses. When I began to understand this principle, it changed everything about the way that I pray, read the Word, and share the gospel with others.

In a nutshell, man is tripartite; we are a spirit, we possess a soul, and we live in a body. The spirit of man is that part of our being that communicates with God. It is our essence. Our soul is our mind, will, and emotions. In Genesis 2:7, the Bible says, *"And the Lord God formed man of the dust of the ground, and breathed into his nostrils the breath of life; and man became a living soul."*

The word *soul* comes from the Hebrew word *nephesh*, which means "living being, seat of emotions and passions, and the activity of the mind" (Strong's H5315). In essence, our soul is where we carry out the human will, reasoning, and emotional intelligence. Finally, the body is what gives the spirit and soul the ability to interact with the physical world. What does this have to do with developing a heavenly vision? Simply stated, we must learn to activate our spiritual senses in order to engage supernatural vision.

In Second Kings 6:17, we see a very remarkable account of the prophet Elisha and his servant Gehazi. The king of Syria was very angry with Elisha because he kept disclosing his every move to his enemy before it happened. I guess this is one of the perks of being a prophet!

FREE E-BOOKS?
YES, PLEASE!

Get **FREE** and deeply discounted **Christian books** for your **e-reader** delivered to your inbox **every week!**

IT'S SIMPLE!

VISIT lovetoreadclub.com

SUBSCRIBE by entering your email address

RECEIVE free and discounted e-book offers and inspiring articles delivered to your inbox every week!

Unsubscribe at any time.

SUBSCRIBE NOW!

LOVE TO READ CLUB

visit **LOVETOREADCLUB.COM** ▶

The king sent chariots and soldiers to surround the city where Elisha was staying.

You are more than a natural person; you are a spiritual being created in the image of God.

Gehazi was afraid because he recognized that he and his master were outnumbered. They appeared to be in grave danger. You can probably imagine the terror and the dread of waking up in the morning only to be surrounded by chariots. Yet in a strange statement, Elisha revealed that there was more to this situation than met the eye. Elisha said, *"Fear not: for they that be with us are more than they that be with them"* (2 Kings 6:16). Then the next verse declares, *"And Elisha prayed, and said, Lord, I pray thee, open his eyes, that he may see. And the Lord opened the eyes of the young man: and he saw: and, behold, the mountain was full of horses and chariots of fire round about Elisha."*

Although in the natural it seemed that they were outnumbered, in the spirit realm they had the advantage. Here is the question: were those angel armies always there, or did they just show up? The only thing that seemed to change was Gehazi's ability to see. What if I told you that there is a host of heavenly armies surrounding you as we speak?

I declare that your spiritual eyes are opened and you are able to see into the spiritual realm. This is a very important component to living in the presence of God, because we cannot live in a reality that we don't recognize and we cannot recognize something of which we have no awareness. God wants us to live in the consciousness of His presence on a daily basis, opening our spiritual eyes to His supernatural reality.

We must ask the Lord to open our spiritual eyes to the reality of the heavenly realm.

FAITH IS THE KEY

One of the keys to living this way is so basic, so simple, that it is often missed or outright dismissed as unimportant and ineffectual. In reality, putting this key into practice releases power beyond what you are able to imagine. You begin to bring heaven down to earth with *your words.* Yes, the very words you speak have the power to manifest the treasures of heaven in your life. Words hold the ability to create or destroy, to speak death or speak life. This is possible because you are made in the image of God and He, the Creator of the entire universe, created the world with His words.

The creation account in the book of Genesis records the words "and God *said*" as He spoke into existence the world we live in and experience today. That's in *your* Bible. Therefore, the power that God displayed when He created the world is the same power that is in you as His highest form of creation. Your mouth is the key to changing your atmosphere.

Words hold more power than most of us realize—more than I am even able to explain. If you truly desire the will of God to be manifested on earth as it is in heaven, your speech must align with the Word of God. Your speech must be in agreement with heaven. The Bible tells us that God's Word is already settled in heaven, which means what He has said is established in heaven. It is in full view in the spiritual realm.

Bringing those things into view in the natural realm, where we physically live, requires alignment with heaven.

As you develop a heavenly vision, seeing the way God sees will become your first nature, not a desperate attempt to try to experience change in your life. If you are going to operate from the vantage point of heaven, seeing things the way God sees them must be your lifestyle. God is consistent; therefore, everything of Him must also be consistent to function effectively because this is the way He created us to be. And yes, you are of Him if you are a born-again believer in Christ.

You may say, "Well I don't know if I can do that, if I can be that disciplined." I assure you that you can because you already are. Consider the everyday things you do on a consistent basis without thinking, whether it's going to work, preparing your children for school, serving in your church, working out, etc. You may think you only do these things because you have to, and that may be true. However, it's no different with God. We *have to be* consistent; we *have to be* expectant; we *have to be* full of faith in God's ability to meet us exactly where we are, every single time.

> What we say affects what we see. If you want to see differently, speak differently.

God isn't fickle. He is consistent, He is faithful, and His faithfulness should compel us to be just like Him. God has given us faith to believe, so believe! The first step to manifesting the kingdom on earth as it is in heaven is by expecting it to happen *when you pray*. It's not for a year from now or next week or even tomorrow. It's for *now*. Now is the time. Now is the day of salvation. *Now* is the moment to live out your faith.

Every moment is the moment to live what you say you believe. When it comes to a lot of the common, everyday things, doing what we believe will get us the results that we need. Even when setbacks show up, we overcome and push past them to reach our goal. Why should we behave any differently when it comes to spiritual benefits? Prayer is the main key, of course, but you must pray and then plug into the benefits of prayer through expectation every single time.

Expectancy is key to receiving what we ask God for. Living and walking in the Holy Spirit requires it. Actively expect God to move on your behalf. The book of James tells us that God is generous, and the Bible is filled with scriptures on God's love, mercy, compassion, concern, regard, and patience for us. Do you know that you have supernatural benefits available to you *right now?*

You must be aware that as a believer in Christ, you don't have to scrape or scramble for anything. All the treasures of heaven are available to you, all the time. That means this very moment in which you are reading, heaven is open to you. Picture Christ in heaven waiting to provide for you. After all, it is through Him that we receive the riches and glory of heaven.

The Bible is filled with examples of Christ meeting the exact expectations of those who believed in Him. He told countless people after having healed them, "Your faith has made you well." Of course, He is the One who provided the healing, but the ones who were seeking Him provided their faith, and the results were wonderful, just as the Scriptures promise.

PRAYER OF ACTIVATION

Father God, help me to see that I am a spiritual being created in Your image. Give me a supernatural vision of a lifestyle spent in Your presence. Open my spiritual eyes to the reality of the heavenly realm. Teach me to speak words of faith that will transform the world I see around me into a representation of Your kingdom of heaven on earth! Amen.

FOR DISCUSSION

1. How can we challenge ourselves to live beyond the "safety net of church as usual" to gain a deeper experience with God?

2. Proverbs 29:18 says, *"Where there is no vision, the people are unrestrained"* (NASB) or, simply put, the people are unchecked, all over the place. What then would be the result of a people with a vision?

3. The Bible has many examples of Christ meeting the *exact* expectations of those who believed Him. Jesus is the One who provides the response. What are we responsible for providing in order to see scriptural promises fulfilled?

CHAPTER 2

THE MOUNTAINTOP EXPERIENCE

*And after six days Jesus taketh Peter, James,
and John his brother, and bringeth them up into
an high mountain apart, and was transfigured
before them: and his face did shine as the sun,
and his raiment was white as the light.*

—MATTHEW 17:1-2

For many years I have been fascinated with the biblical account often referred to as the mountain of transfiguration. In the Gospel of Matthew, Jesus took His disciples (namely Peter, James, and John) to a high mountain and was transfigured before them. Later in the account, Moses and Elijah appeared and Peter offered to build three tabernacles—one for Jesus, one for Moses, and one for Elijah. Who wouldn't want to bask in this wonderful presence forever? However, I believe that there is more to this story than meets the eye. What if I told you that within the crevices of this biblical account lie secrets for personal revival and awakening?

The mountaintop experience as recorded in Matthew's Gospel was much more than a historical event; it was a supernatural pattern for the New Testament believer. You see, God is a God of patterns. If we look closely, we will notice that as soon as they came down from the mountaintop experience, there was a demonic oppression waiting for them in the valley. Why is this so important to note?

Many believers think that an encounter with God exempts them from spiritual opposition. These are people I refer to as revival junkies. They are constantly going from encounter to encounter trying to find spiritual bliss that will create for them a utopian reality where they don't have to deal with anything or anyone. If left up to them, they would soak into eternity. But the truth of the matter is that God allows us to have mountaintop encounters with Him in order to equip us for the valley.

Essentially, Jesus was trying to teach His disciples to live *from* the mountain, not *for* the mountain. Are you living for the mountain or from the mountain? The answer to this question will determine your capacity for supernatural life.

While it is true that God is a God of encounters, it is also true that God is a God of pattern. A pattern is simply a systematic way of doing things. The kingdom of God has a pattern. For example, the Bible says, *"But seek ye first the kingdom of God, and his righteousness; and all these things shall be added unto you"* (Matt. 6:33). As long as a person seeks things before they seek the kingdom, they will never attain what they're searching for. Conversely, if we seek first the kingdom we are posturing ourselves to receive everything that we truly desire.

Jesus didn't seek the mountaintop; He sought the presence of the Father!

THE SPIRIT OF AWAKENING

It is evident that the Church is in desperate need of an awakening. What do I mean by *awakening?* This is a point I want to share with a powerful testimony of my own encounter with the presence of God.

Years ago, I found myself in a very desperate place spiritually. I was burned out, frustrated, and tired. Church as usual had become so mundane and boring. My wife and I were frustrated from all of the spiritual opposition we were experiencing in ministry while at the same time trying to balance the needs of a growing family. To be honest with you, I really didn't even have a prayer life anymore. My time with God was mechanical at best. Yet deep within there was a longing for more.

I was so hungry for the presence and power of God in my life. I wanted to experience Him the way that I had when I was just a young teenager. One day while earnestly praying to God and asking Him for personal revival, I cried out of the depths of my spirit. Honestly, I didn't really feel anything. All of a sudden, I saw in a vision an angel standing behind me, holding a bucket of water.

This angel proceeded to pour the water on top of my head, and as soon as the water touched my head I jumped up off of the ground and I began to run. I was literally awakened by this icy cold shock. Immediately, I began praying in tongues. I felt a jolt of energy flow through my body. It was as if I was hit with 10,000 volts of electricity all at once. I began to pray like never before.

I asked this angel what his name was; he said to me, "My name is Joy." I was literally awakened by the power of God. Just as I experienced a personal awakening, I believe it's time for the body of Christ to experience a collective awakening. An awakening is not just an event; it is a reality. Awakening is the act of suddenly becoming aware of something.

> There is an awareness of the presence of God coming to the body of Christ like never before.

I believe there is an awakening of consciousness that is going to take place in the Church that will usher us into the greatest move of signs and wonders and miracles in the earth. We will literally see this happening before our very eyes. People from all over the world will be pouring into churches to experience a touch from God. I don't think this is something relegated to a city, region, or territory, but I believe this is a coming global reality. As I travel the globe, I am sensing a hunger and a thirst for the presence that I have never seen before; it's as if there is a sovereign recalibration taking place.

THE MYSTERY OF THE FIG TREE

There is a very powerful account found in the Gospel of Mark that illustrates the power of this move of the Spirit of God. The Bible records:

> *And seeing a fig tree afar off having leaves, he came, if haply he might find any thing thereon: and when he came to it, he found nothing but leaves; for the time of figs was*

not yet. And Jesus answered and said unto it, No man eat fruit of thee hereafter for ever. And his disciples heard it (Mark 11:13-14).

There is a portion of the verse that we cannot ignore that says, *"For the time of figs was not yet."* What does this mean? In other words, it was not the season for the fig harvest, yet Jesus expected fruit to be on the tree. It would be safe to assume that Jesus knew what time the fig tree was supposed to produce, yet He cursed the tree for not having fruit in the wrong season. This is a mystery about the Church.

For the last 1,500 years, the Church has been seasonal in her thinking. In other words, we have had a tendency to lock God into seasons of movement, and when there is no movement we attribute it to the wrong season. Jesus forever cursed the mindset of seasonal productivity. We often hear leaders say that we must wait for revival to hit. They are eagerly anticipating God's next season of revival and awakening. But I want to submit to you that revival and awakening is now.

Jesus gave us a pattern to follow. This pattern shows us that the magnitude of the fruit we produce is not determined by the season we are in but by the revelation we possess. This tells us that anytime the presence of God is manifested, it is harvest time. Don't wait for your season to change, engage the presence of Jesus now.

THE POWER OF NOW

The mountain of transfiguration gives us a perfect picture of the heavenly realm and the power of now. What do I mean by the power of now? I will explain in a moment. When Peter saw this miraculous event take place, his first instinct was to build tabernacles on the mountain. In other words, he wanted to build a residence in this magnificent encounter. Before we look down on Peter's zeal and enthusiasm, we must examine ourselves.

It is human nature to abide in the most blissful state possible. We tend to build comfort zones in the places that give us the most peace and gratification, whether it is in a church service, a conference, an experience, or even a relationship. We have a habit of recreating and mechanizing experiences. In the modern Church, we have become experts at creating the right lighting and singing the right songs, all in an effort to recapture a particular experience.

Peter wanted to build a timeshare around the supernatural experience he had just witnessed. I am assuming that he would have attempted to visit those tabernacles from time to time. Yet our Lord never acknowledges his request. Why? It was never the intent of God for us to recreate an experience but to be a living host of His presence. *We* are the tabernacles. The Bible says, *"What? know ye not that your body is the temple of the Holy Ghost which is in you, which ye have of God, and ye are not your own?"* (1 Cor. 6:19). God does not want us to settle for spiritual nostalgia; He wants us to live in the realm called *now.* You see, God is eternal, and as a result He constantly resides in the eternal now. In other words, He is not going to do anything; He has already done everything. We simply enter into the reality of what He has done by faith. We are not waiting on God; He is waiting on us, in a sense.

> When we learn to live in the now, we learn to live in the realm of **unlimited possibilities.**

Most believers have no concept of the realm of *now*. This is why you often hear people say, "I remember when God moved in Brownsville," or "I remember what God did in Toronto." Don't get me wrong—there is nothing wrong with honoring and appreciating past encounters with God or even building off of them, but we must be careful not to be locked into the past. Jesus wanted the revelation of His splendor to leave an indelible mark on the hearts and minds of His disciples so that they would have a permanent touch point for the reality of God's presence.

The problem is that we live in a society that is always disconnected from the now. In fact, we are very rarely in the present. We are either thinking about the past or we are obsessing over the future. Instead of entering into the reality of the manifest presence of God, Peter was already trying to figure out how he was going to recreate this awesome experience.

> God never reveals anything to you that He doesn't invite you to enter into.

Now is not the past and it is not the future; it is now! It is *the present time or moment.* Jesus invited the disciples into the eternal now to see things the way they really are from heaven's perspective. Until this time, they saw Jesus as a rabbi and teacher, but on the mountain they received a glimpse into the heavenly realm. They saw the glory! What if this was not an isolated event but a regular occurrence that Jesus invited His disciples into? I am not going to speculate, but it is an interesting consideration.

LIVING IN THE NOW

Jesus called His disciples into a *kairos* (now) moment on the mountain top. This was not to entertain them, but it was an invitation into an eternal reality where Jesus was glorified. He wanted them to *see* something that would resonate within them for the rest of their lives and ministries. This encounter was so significant that it shaped the apostle Peter's consciousness for the rest of his ministry. This is evidenced in Second Peter 1:17-18:

> *For he received from God the Father honour and glory, when there came such a voice to him from the excellent glory, This is my beloved Son, in whom I am well pleased. And this voice which came from heaven we heard, when we were with him in the holy mount.*

Peter was an eyewitness of the majesty of Jesus. He heard the Father speak out of the glory and declare that Christ was His Son. This was a prophetic moment of revelation. This should signify to us that the presence of God is not a place of speculation but a place of revelation.

Mountaintop encounters alter our vision and usher us into supernatural realities.

God always reveals things in His presence, and revelation changes our identity and the way we see the world around us. The disciples could never un-see what they saw on the mountaintop.

Jesus was inviting the disciples to live in the supernatural now, a place of revelation and power. Once we live in the now, we are no longer bound by the circumstances of our lives. This is why Jesus told His disciples to take no thought for their lives. Why? Whatever you think on, you focus on, and whatever you focus on, you gravitate toward.

Every time we consciously enter into the presence of God, we are entering the realm of now. There is no worry or fear in that place. The problem is that we can't always sit in a revival service 24 hours a day. So what do we do? We must learn to live *from* the presence. The disciples were called into a reality that would change their thoughts and perceptions of everything. It was a place of identity and affirmation.

Jesus was affirmed in the glory. In the same manner, we are affirmed in the presence of God. We hear His voice and are affirmed in our authority as sons and daughters of the Most High. We must take this revelation and appropriate it in every area of our lives. When we see a demon in the valley, we can be reminded of who we are in heaven and the authority that we possess.

TRANSFORMED BY THE PRESENCE

As we mentioned earlier, God lives in the place called *the eternal now*. He doesn't just see and know everything in time, but time is inside of Him. It is His creation. Why is this so important? Because when we encounter God, we encounter eternity. Every time we enter into God's presence or His presence enters the room, eternity invades time.

The law of environment says that your environment will change you before you change it. In other words, eternity is greater than time; therefore, it has the power to transform us. You cannot encounter God's presence and remain the same.

We said earlier that the mountain of transfiguration was a heavenly pattern for intimacy and authority in the earth. We also must experience a transfiguration in the presence of God. The word *transfiguration* comes from the Greek word *metamorphoō*, which means to be transformed or to undergo a metamorphosis (Strong's G3339). This is the same word used in Romans 12:1-2:

> *I beseech you therefore, brethren, by the mercies of God, that ye present your bodies a living sacrifice, holy, acceptable unto God, which is your reasonable service. And be not conformed to this world: but be ye transformed by the renewing of your mind, that ye may prove what is that good, and acceptable, and perfect, will of God.*

God has called every believer to experience a transfiguration in the sense that our minds and lifestyles experience a metamorphosis by the presence and power of God. That's right! The presence of God should transform us. One of the greatest tragedies in the modern Church is the tendency to seek an experience with God that we have no intention of allowing to change us.

God is not just interested in revival as we have defined it (great music, crying, worshiping, and laughing); He is interested in transforming the culture in the earth. How does He accomplish this? By transforming His children into His image and giving them the power and the authority to transform the world around them. In other words, you are transformed to be a transformer. We must be intentional about change. Every time we encounter God's presence, He desires to reveal something to us that will change us.

One day while I was in a worship service, the Lord began to open my eyes in the spirit realm. I saw angels placing gifts underneath the seats of those worshiping. These were no ordinary gifts! They were gemstones the size of a person's head. They came in all shapes and colors.

Then I noticed something even more astounding. The people worshiping were completely oblivious to what was taking place. They were singing songs about God being an awesome provider and a miracle worker, yet they had no awareness that He was manifesting the very things they prayed about while they were worshiping Him. This is due to the fact that we really don't know what worship is or what it is about.

The first occurrence of the word *worship* is in Genesis 22:5. Abraham was told by God to sacrifice his only son Isaac, and when he spoke to his servants he told them that he was going to worship. Why? It was understood at that time that there was no worship without sacrifice. Every time we come before God in worship, it requires a sacrifice. The reason we can approach God in worship without the sense of guilt or shame is because God sacrificed His own Son to bring us into fellowship with Himself. However, this goes even deeper.

Worship is more than an experience; it is a lifestyle of supernatural expectation.

The word worship used here is *shachah*, and it means to bow or make obeisance (Strong's H7812). It is a posture of submission and total dependence on God. It is a posture of expectancy from the One you are worshiping. In other words, you cannot separate your worship from your expectation. Worship without expectancy is like a song without sound, yet there are millions of Christians who come before God with no expectation.

EMPOWERED FOR THE VALLEY

The mountaintop encounter with Jesus was a temporary experience that was designed to invoke a lifestyle of the supernatural. We see that the moment the disciples came down from the mountain with Jesus, they encountered demonic powers. The boy oppressed by demons could not find any relief (see Matt. 17:15-18). The father of this boy cried out to Jesus and asked Him to heal the son because the disciples were also unable to get results. Jesus then called His own disciples faithless and perverse and asked a very interesting question: "How long shall I be with you?" In other words, "I have been with you for all of this time, and you still don't get it!"

> The Mountain reveals the Son of God, but the valley reveals the Son of Man. That which was revealed in the mountain was demonstrated in the valley.

The disciples didn't realize that they had been resourced by heaven and that they could use the empowerment and authority to deal with any and every evil that would seek to resist them. They had been conformed but not transformed. Jesus ushered His disciples into a powerful reality of worship and revelation. The mountaintop encounter was, in fact, an empowerment for the valley. As we ascend in worship, adoration, and revelation, we descend with power and authority. We are given the responsibility to subdue every other domain through the revelation that we receive from God.

Every time God speaks to you, it's an invitation to an eternal reality. His spoken word to you is an invitation to another dimension.

PRAYER OF ACTIVATION

Father God, give me a new awareness of Your presence, and teach me to live with You in the eternal now. Reveal to me the realm of unlimited possibilities that come from living out of Your presence. Transform me with a lifestyle of worship and supernatural expectation. I take Your invitation and enter into the eternal now with You! Amen.

FOR DISCUSSION

1. In the example of the fig tree, Jesus cursed the mindset of seasonal productivity. The magnitude of the fruit we possess is not determined by season but by the revelation we possess. What does this tell us about any time the manifested presence of God takes place?

2. God constantly resides in the eternal now. He is not going to do anything. He has already done everything. What happens when we learn to live in the now?

3. God always reveals things in His presence. The disciples could never un-see what they saw on the mountaintop. What do mountaintop experiences do to your vision?

PRACTICUM

Consider that there is an intense recalibration, an extreme awakening happening now to ensure that the children of God receive the presence of God such as never before. Think about the fact that it is human nature to abide in the most blissful state possible; specifically, it is human nature to want to be at ease and comfortable, even if it means stagnation. What if God is working to shake you from your past or your comfortable, "I've always done it this way" to give you an "at the present moment"—a heavenly perspective or a revelation from His presence that impels movement? How does that sense of urgency from God affect your choice to live *through* His revelation—comfortable receipt of information—or *from* the reality and revelation His presence declares? Is your comfort that important?

CHAPTER 3

CREATED FOR INTIMACY

And this is life eternal, that they might know thee the only true God, and Jesus Christ, whom thou hast sent.

—JOHN 17:3

One of the most powerful gospels is the Gospel of John. It is considered by many scholars to be an ontological book. The focus of this Gospel is the nature and identity of Jesus. John 1 starts off by telling us that *"In the beginning was the Word, and the Word was with God, and the Word was God"* (John 1:1). Throughout this Gospel, we see themes such as eternal life, truth, resurrection, and knowing God.

The Bible says, *"And this is life eternal, that they might know thee the only true God, and Jesus Christ, whom thou hast sent"* (John 17:3).

For many years, it has been taught that we will one day enter eternal life. When I was growing up, I would hear gospel songs that would talk about the sweet by and by. Though there is some truth to this (we will enter the kingdom of heaven at the end of the age), it was extremely incomplete.

The gospel is not about entering into eternal life; it is about eternal life entering into us. The moment we become born again, we receive the gift of eternal life. *Eternal life* comes from the Greek word *zoe*, which means life to the full and overflowing, the very life of God (Strong's G2222). In other words, God has given us the same life that He has in Himself.

This is not simply about entering heaven one day; it's about possessing intimate knowledge of the Father. Looking at John 17:3 again, the word *know* comes from an interesting Greek word—*ginosko*, which means intimate, experiential knowledge (Strong's G1097). It is a Jewish idiom for intercourse. God doesn't just want us to know about Him; He wants us to *know* Him deeply and intimately. In fact, we were created for intimacy. Still, what does it mean to know Him? We said that the word *know* comes from the idiomatic expression for intimacy. Adam *knew* Eve his wife and she conceived (see Gen. 4:1). Knowing is not determined by the concepts we grasp but by the conception that takes place within us.

Now before the males get uncomfortable about conceiving, we are talking in a spiritual sense here. Our mind and consciousness are transformed by what we know just as much as a woman is transformed spiritually, physically, and emotionally as a result of her pregnancy. Intimacy is much more about relationship than it is ritual, and this relationship must produce something tangible within our lives.

BIRTHING THE MIRACULOUS

I will never forget the first time my wife was pregnant. It was the most exciting and frightening thing I had ever experienced up until that point. I was constantly aware of the fact that our lives would never be the same after our daughter was born. I knew it meant more responsibility and more accountability.

Unfortunately, my wife experienced many complications during her first pregnancy. Toward the end of her last trimester, the doctors were very concerned about the birth weight of the baby. As a result of their concern, they scheduled my wife for an induction (chemically inducing the delivery). This process greatly increased the risk of a C-section. When my wife went into the hospital for the induction, I expected her to come back out in a few hours with a baby in her hands. Apparently, it didn't work like that in real life.

Hours of labor went by and there was no sign of my wife even dilating, to say nothing of the baby coming. Twenty-four hours went by and nothing was happening. I decided to pray at this point. I asked God what was going on, and in the midst of my inquiry a boldness came over me that I cannot really explain. Immediately, the doctors came in and told us that they were going to perform a C-section if my wife didn't start dilating soon. That was my cue!

I told the doctor to give us one hour, and I guaranteed them that they would see significant progress by the time they came back in the room. I prayed harder and more earnestly than I had ever prayed in my life. I declared, "Baby, it's time for you to come out now. Daddy's waiting!" Within the hour, the doctor came back in the room ready to perform a C-section, and when they checked my wife's cervix they yelled, "The baby's head is poking out!" Thus, my wife delivered our oldest daughter.

While sitting in the delivery room reflecting, the Lord spoke to me and said, "Your wife was not the only one giving birth." While my wife was giving birth to a physical baby girl, I was birthing something miraculous. I went to another level in prayer as a result of seeing what God was able to do. He revealed Himself to me in a new way, and this resulted in a greater knowledge of who He was and is.

> **G**od has not just called you and me to see miracles but to birth the miraculous.

For many people, Christianity is merely a spiritual spectator sport. They see it as a series of events on their journey to heaven. Nothing could be further from the truth. The only way to know God is to engage our faith and action in a very deliberate way. The more we experience Him the more we know Him, and the more we know Him the more we experience Him. This is the cycle that we should all be in!

I challenge you to change your approach to the things of God. Instead of looking for a miracle, give birth to one. Whatever God can get through you He can get to you! God has called us to birth the miraculous life the Word of God promises us. The Bible says, *"Then said Jesus to those Jews which believed on him, If ye continue in my word, then are ye my disciples indeed; and ye shall know the truth, and the truth shall make you free"* (John 8:31-32).

As we allow God's Word to take control of our lives, His truth takes root in us and that root produces fruit—that fruit is freedom. I often tell people that if they want to see change or breakthrough in a certain area of their lives, the key is to continue in God's Word in that particular area. When it comes to walking in intimacy and authority, we must meditate on who the Word of God says we are and what the Word says we possess. You will never walk in the manifestation of a truth you do not know.

PRAYER OF ACTIVATION

Father God, I want to experience intimacy in my relationship with You. Show me how to remove the rituals and truly know You in a way that reproduces tangible results within me. Allow me to birth the miraculous for You. Guide me with Your Word so that I continue as Your disciple and Your truth makes me free! Amen.

FOR DISCUSSION

1. What does it mean to birth the miraculous?

2. What is the key if you want to see change or break-through in a certain area of your life?

CHAPTER 4

BEYOND THE VEIL

And, behold, the veil of the temple was rent
in twain from the top to the bottom; and
the earth did quake, and the rocks rent.
—MATTHEW 27:51

I n the western world, we often take the concept of worship for granted. But in the Old Testament, the ramifications of worship were very clear. One wrong move or violation of the laws that governed the Tabernacle could cost you your life. You see, God is holy! But what does this mean?

The word *holiness* comes from the Hebrew word *qodesh*, which literally means sacredness or apartness (Strong's H6918). God is set apart from any and everything that is unclean. The Bible tells us that God is light, and in Him is no darkness. This is the very reason why the Tabernacle required a veil.

God had to separate the Holy of Holies from the inner court and the outer court. Only the high priest could enter into the Holy of Holies once a year. This was known as *Yom Kippur* or the Day of Atonement. Under the old covenant, only the high priest could speak in the Holy of Holies on behalf of the people. This priest was seen as holy and separate from the rest of the congregation.

In the new covenant, Jesus Christ is our high priest who went beyond the veil on our behalf to consecrate for us a new and living way. As a result of His atoning work on the cross and His resurrection from the dead, you and I can live a lifestyle beyond the veil. That means that we have access to face-to-face intimacy with God, 24 hours a day. Unfortunately, many Christians today are living a lifestyle that is relegated to an outer-court encounter. They pray to God when they go to church and they read the Bible when they go to Bible study, yet deep within the recesses of their heart they are longing for so much more.

What if I told you that you could live from the holy place? Remember, an encounter with God is not an event but a lifestyle! What if I told you that Sunday mornings don't have to be the height of your spiritual experience? This is not to say that Sunday is not an important time of the week to worship, as is any day that you choose to worship. But it is to say that God did not call us to live for Sundays; He has called us to live out every day of the week as a Son-day!

THE VEIL OF RELIGION AND TRADITION

What if I told you that the biggest threat to living out the fullness of the Christian life was not the devil? What if I told you that the greatest obstacle to your progress and the things of God was not spiritual warfare?

In my many years of ministry, I have found that the biggest threat to supernatural living is a religious spirit. Let me define what I mean by *religious spirit*. We know from Scripture that religion is a good thing. This is what the apostle James calls true religion: it is to visit the widow and the fatherless. It is to keep ourselves unspotted from the contamination of this world. It is to operate in the love of God and Christian compassion daily. This is not what I am referring to by the term *religious spirit*.

The word *religion* is derived from the Latin *religio*, which means an obligation or bond. It was used in the old days to refer to life under monastic vows. Monks stayed within the confines of the monastery to carry out their vows to God. Jesus addressed negative religion in the Gospel accounts. In Matthew 6:5, Jesus said, *"Thou shalt not be as the hypocrites are: for they love to pray standing in the synagogues and in the corners of the streets, that they may be seen of men. Verily I say unto you, They have their reward."*

In other words, many of the religious leaders during the time of Jesus were bound to their traditions. Their religious experience did not go beyond the four walls of the synagogue. Many people today are bound by a religious spirit in the sense that they cannot see their spiritual life beyond the four walls of the church. Yet Matthew 28:19 tells us to go into all the world.

We were never instructed to stay within the four walls of the church. Can you imagine parking your car at the gas station and never turning the ignition and driving anywhere? This is exactly what many people do every single week. They park their faith at the church every Sunday and leave it there, not realizing that the church was designed to be a refueling and empowerment station, not a parking lot. God does not want us to live a stagnant Christian life, but an active and vibrant lifestyle of faith, filled with His supernatural power.

ENLIGHTEN YOUR UNDERSTANDING

Many years ago, while praying and spending time with God, the Lord gave me a vision. In this vision, I saw an angel who was about 15 feet tall. He was massive. He wore a gold belt and a crown upon his head. He also had a sword attached to his waist. If you ever needed a security guard, this was your man! In this vision I thought to myself, "What a mighty angel this is!"

Immediately, I heard the Lord say, "That's not an angel; that's you!" I was absolutely shocked. I never considered the fact that from God's perspective, we are kings and priests in the earth.

We have been called by God to carry out His eternal agenda in the earth realm. But this can only take place when we enter into the consciousness of who we really are, and that consciousness comes as a result of moving beyond the veil of religion and tradition into a place of intimacy and power. We are not spiritual couch potatoes waiting for Jesus to crack the sky. We are spiritual ambassadors invested with the full power and authority of the kingdom of God. So what are you waiting for?

It would be enough for God to have given us His power and His authority, but He didn't stop there—He gave us His presence. The greatest gift God can give to any person is His presence! Jesus said that He came to seek and to save that which was lost. Many have taught that man lost his authority in the Garden of Eden. Though this is true, it is incomplete.

The human race did not just lose their authority in the Garden of Eden; they lost God's presence. This is why Adam and Eve were aware that they were naked after they ate from the tree of the knowledge of good and evil. The Bible says that their eyes were opened and they knew that they were naked. Yet, in the previous chapter of Genesis, the Bible tells us that they were already naked. What changed? The glory of God was their covering. Once they ate from the tree that was forbidden, they lost the glory.

Jesus came to the earth not only to redeem man and restore his authority in the earth, but He also came to restore the glory of God to the human race. Through Jesus we have access to the Holy of Holies—a place where the manifest presence of God dwells. This place is no longer contained within a physical ark; it dwells within each and every believer who calls upon the name of Jesus as their Lord and Savior. How do we respond to this truth? The answer is, we must open the eyes of our understanding.

This is the prayer that Paul prayed in Ephesians 1:18: *"The eyes of your understanding being enlightened; that ye may know what is the hope of his calling, and what the riches of the glory of his inheritance in the saints."* In other words, the apostle Paul was letting us know that the key to experiencing the full manifestation of God's power in our lives is being enlightened to the truth that God's glory resides within us. Once we get a glimpse of this revelation, we plug into God's eternal power. You will never look at yourself the same way once you realize how much glory resides within you. Your life will experience a radical shift!

GOD'S TREASURE CHEST

Growing up, I can remember watching pirate movies. The pirates would sail the seven seas looking for hidden treasure. Usually once they landed on an island, they would look for a treasure chest. This was simply a fancy word for a box full of gold and precious stones. In most cases, the pirates would not have the key. So once they found the treasure chest they also had to look for the key or find some other way to break it open, because only the owner of the treasure chest has access to the contents therein.

We are God's treasure chest. We are the vessels God has placed His eternal treasures within. This is why the enemy has fought you so long and so hard—because he knows what lies within you. The question is, do *you* know what lies within you?

It would be extremely unfair for God to show you that you were a treasure chest and not give you the keys to unlock that treasure. Make no mistake, the treasure belongs to God, but the contents He has placed within you. How do we access this treasure? In Matthew 16:19, Jesus said *"And I will give unto thee the keys of the kingdom of heaven: and whatsoever thou shalt bind on earth shall be bound in heaven: and whatsoever thou shalt loose on earth shall be loosed in heaven."*

In the Greek, the word for "key" implies that which gives access to various doors. In other words, a key is meant to open something. The Bible tells us that whatever we bind on earth shall be bound in heaven and whatever we loose on the earth shall be loosed in heaven. The word *loose* here means to untie or to release. What does God want us to release? He wants us to release what is in heaven.

The Bible says, *"Thy will be done in earth, as it is in heaven"* (Matt. 6:10). Therefore, we know it is God's will for His reality in heaven to be our reality on the earth. Many people are frustrated because they are not seeing revival even though they pray for that every week. The truth is, God never told us to pray for revival; He told us to release it.

The word *revive* means "to make alive." Heaven is already alive! Therefore, the key to global revival is to get what is in heaven into the earth. My friends, you and I are the treasure chest where God has hidden revival and awakening for the people around us. Now is the time for us to unlock our treasure chest and release the treasure within. The key is revelation. The word *revelation* simply means unveiling. It means to pull back the curtain and to reveal what is already present.

Revelation is twofold. First, God must reveal to us who *He* is. Second, God must reveal to us who *we* are. Jesus told Peter, *"Flesh and blood hath not revealed it unto thee, but my Father which is in heaven"* (Matt 16:17). Once Peter received the revelation of who Jesus was, he was able to receive the revelation of who *he* was. Your identity is attached to your revelation. Every time God reveals Himself to us, a key is turned within our heart unlocking the treasure within.

Years ago, I was in Australia ministering in the capital, Sydney. There was a young lady who came to one of my meetings. The Lord gave me a prophetic word for her. He told me to tell her that she would become a great worship leader. As I shared the word the Lord had given me for her, she immediately began to contend with me. She exclaimed with great passion, "No, no, no, no, you have the wrong person. I don't even know how to sing."

After she was done arguing with me, I insisted on the original word that God had given me. I told her again, "God says you're going to be a great worship leader." Moments later, she began to laugh. After she was done laughing, the presence of God began to touch her. She began to weep. She began to cry. Soon, she fell under the power of God.

Why did she respond this way? She was focused on the treasure chest and the way it looked rather than the treasure on the inside. God always hides His greatest treasures in earthen vessels.

Days later, I went back to the church in Sydney. When I entered into the service that night, guess who I saw leading worship? It was the very lady I prophesied to days before. She was lifting her voice releasing the most beautiful worship I had heard up until that point. What happened?

The treasure was always there, but she didn't have the key. When I spoke a prophetic word over her life by revelation, she received the key that she needed to unlock the treasure of worship God deposited within her. *"But we have this treasure in earthen vessels, that the excellency of the power may be of God, and not of us"* (2 Cor. 4:7). The keys of the kingdom always come in the form of revelation. Sometimes, we fail to realize the magnitude of God's power within us.

THE CLAY POT GENERATION

In Genesis 2, the Bible says *"And the Lord God formed man of the dust of the ground, and breathed into his nostrils the breath of life; and man became a living soul"* (Gen. 2:7). Interestingly enough, the name *Adam* actually means dirt or red clay. It is fascinating to consider that the first artist to ever create a sculpture was God. He sculpted man from the dust of the ground and formed him perfectly in His own image; then He gave man the greatest gift He could give to any being in the universe—His Spirit.

Can you imagine that God entrusted the most precious thing in the cosmos to a clay pot? It is clear from Scripture that God specializes in hiding Himself in the simplest of things. God called Noah to build a boat out of wood to preserve the human race. God raised up a simple man from the land of the Chaldeans and called him to be the father of many nations. God took an old, beat-up shepherd's staff and used it to deliver the Israelites out of Egypt. He took a retired prince of Egypt with a stuttering problem and used him to pronounce His word of deliverance to Pharaoh. The Son of God was clothed in humanity and placed in a manger. It is clear that we serve a God who knows how to hide Himself in the simplest of things.

This current generation is what I call the "clay pot" generation. In other words, this is a generation that does not know the magnitude of what God desires to do through them. Yet God is ready and willing to raise up jars of clay to s"how forth His glory. Unfortunately, many people get so caught up in the look of the pot that they ignore the treasure it holds. I want to let you know that *"greater is he that is in you, than he that is in the world"* (1 John 4:4). The Spirit of the living God dwells on the inside of you; therefore, you are not ordinary or typical.

> You are an extraordinary people who serve an extraordinary God who has called you to carry out an extraordinary assignment.

THE MYSTERY OF THE
WOODEN CHALICE

One of my favorite movies is *Indiana Jones and the Raiders of the Lost Ark*. In this blockbuster hit, Indiana Jones is searching for what he believes is a fountain of eternal life. According to the narrative of the movie, the Crusaders hid an ancient relic that held the key to living forever.

In one very important scene of the film, the ghost of an ancient Crusader is talking to Indiana Jones and giving him the opportunity to choose the chalice of Jesus. The ghost says to him "choose wisely." The first man chose the most luxurious chalice in the room laden with gold and precious stones. As he drank from this beautiful cup, it was evident that he had made a grave mistake, and as a result he fell dead.

When it was Indiana Jones's turn to choose the chalice of Jesus, he went to the back of the room and chose an old wooden cup. This was clearly the cup of a carpenter. As he drank from this old wooden cup, the Crusader looked at him and said, "You've chosen wisely." What can we gather from this fictitious story?

Supernatural things often come in natural packaging. As you are reading this book, you may be saying to yourself, "But I'm not a dynamic speaker, pastor, or successful businessperson." The truth is, God does not need dynamic to demonstrate His power. All He needs is a willing vessel. Will you be the wooden chalice in the hand of Jesus? Will you be the one He can use to pour out His glory on a lost and dying generation?

PRAYER OF ACTIVATION

Lord, help me to enlighten my understanding to see beyond the veil of religion and tradition. Reveal to me the treasure You have hidden within me. Show me the true treasures within the people around me so that we are not blinded by the clay pots we appear to be on the surface. Amen.

FOR DISCUSSION

1. What is the biggest obstacle to your progress in the things of God and supernatural living?

2. Revelation means to unveil or to reveal what is already present. Revelation from God is twofold. What are the two things that God must reveal to man?

3. You have been called by God to carry out His eternal
    agenda in the earth realm. What must you do for this
    to take place?

CHAPTER 5

MORE THAN RELIGION

*For I say unto you, That except your
righteousness shall exceed the righteousness
of the scribes and Pharisees, ye shall in no
case enter into the kingdom of heaven.*

—MATTHEW 5:20

What if I told you that being a Christian was much more than a religion? In fact, what if I told you that being a believer in Jesus Christ was not a religion at all? How would that change your worldview? The first thing we should do at this point is define the word *religion*. Religion is defined as a particular system of faith and worship.

In other words, religion is mankind's attempt to package God and His ways into a system that can be replicated and executed.

When most people think of religion, they think of a set of regulations that one must follow to be found acceptable to the Creator. According to this definition, there would be many religions out there, all with their own system of worship, their own approach to the deity of their choice. Some emphasize spiritual enlightenment. Others focus on the reconciliation of human relationships. There are even religions that focus on the preservation of the earth. Now that we have provided a general definition of religion, we can see that being a believer in Christ does not necessarily fall into this category (we will speak of this in more detail in Chapter 11).

Yes, there are tenets to the Christian faith as well as practices of worship, but being a believer in Jesus Christ is so much more. In fact, the word *Christian* literally means "imitator of Christ." When was the last time you thought of yourself as an imitator of Jesus? This idea is not just that of following someone's actions but, in fact, having that person's same nature. Now before I go on, I want to explain this concept a bit further. In the book of Acts 11:26, we see this account:

> *And when he had found him, he brought him unto Antioch. And it came to pass, that a whole year they assembled themselves with the church, and taught much people. And the disciples were called Christians first in Antioch.*

The first time believers in Christ were referred to as Christians was in the city of Antioch. This was a term that non-believers used to articulate their perception of believers in Jesus. There was something about the early Church that reminded everyone around them of Jesus Christ. In the same way a son reminds people of his father or a daughter her mother, we the Church should be an expression and a reminder to the world that Jesus is alive.

In this we are "Jesus imitators," for lack of a better word. This idea goes far beyond the concept of religion. Being a Christian is a matter of identity, not ritual. The more conscious we are of this reality, the more successfully we are positioned to live the Christian life. So you may ask, how does that make Christianity more than a religion? Simple—we are not commanded to live for God or complete a set of tasks that please Him, but we are commanded to allow Christ to live in and through us. In Galatians 2:20, Paul says:

> *I am crucified with Christ: nevertheless I live; yet not I, but Christ liveth in me: and the life which I now live in the flesh I live by the faith of the Son of God, who loved me, and gave himself for me.*

Paul says that Christ is alive and active inside of him. It is not him trying to attain to God's standard, but it is the power of the Holy Spirit resident in Paul that enables him to become everything that God intended for him to be. This is so much more than a system of worship; this is a living relationship with a living Jesus that changes every dynamic of our life.

We cannot come to Christ by faith and remain the same. It is impossible! If we could only grasp this simple concept that Jesus is not a list of dos and don'ts, but He is God incarnate who died on the cross for our sins! He died to restore us back to right fellowship with the Father and bring us to a place where God could be made manifest in us. In the Old Testament, God dwelt in physical infrastructures such as the Tabernacle and the Ark of the Covenant; but in the New Testament, God makes our spirit man His dwelling place. We are the temple of the Holy Spirit!

Paul goes further to assert that he is crucified with Christ. This is another one of those ontological realities mentioned earlier. What Paul is saying is that in a metaphysical sense his old, unregenerate man was nailed to the cross with Jesus and put to death once and for all.

The former Paul is no more. He is dead! The new man is full of Jesus Christ—so much so that Paul says that we live by the very faith of Christ, not faith in Christ! We live by the very faith that Christ has. This faith is produced in us by God's Spirit. This is what being a Christian is all about.

THE GREAT AWAKENING

In the early 1800s, there was what was known as a Great Awakening in American church culture. This was a time of dynamic preaching and great revival among churches, evangelists, and Christian missionaries. This Great Awakening shaped the very fabric of America. Thousands of people came to faith in Christ, and many organizations were born out of this time. There was a revisiting of biblical fundamentals. God used many men and women mightily during this time.

I believe there is an even greater awakening that is available to the Church at large once we realize that being a Christian is not a religious exercise. With all the *great awakenings* in church history, we still seem to omit the simple aspect of having a relationship with God and becoming a new creation. When we realize the very essence of salvation, then we will see that it affects every single area of our lives.

God wants to awaken a deeper desire for Himself in our generation. He wants us to know that being a believer is not for religious people; it is for people who have failed, people who have been broken, and people who need to be restored. Why is this good news? It is good news because it lets us know that we don't have to be religious to walk in covenant relationship with God. There is a power in relating to our heavenly Father on the basis of what He has done and not what we can do.

RELIGION BASED ON WORKS

What we quickly realize when we look at religion is that it is all about our own ability. It is about how well we execute and how consistently we perform, but this is a path to frustration and stagnation. Jesus is a living, breathing person who desires to make His abode inside of us. He is the one with the power. When we yield ourselves to this living, all-powerful person, that very power is released in and through us.

The world doesn't need another religion; they have plenty. What the world actually needs is to see the living Christ. When they see Him for who He really is, they will be drawn to Him with awe and wonder. Religion stands in the way of our ability to see God and to demonstrate Him to others. Why is there such a strong temptation to be religious in our culture? Simple—man desires to be glorified. It is pride!

Somewhere along the way, we were told that God is looking at our good behavior as a measuring tool for His faithfulness in our life. We think we will receive "points" if we can perform the right way, when in reality God is not looking at our performance at all; He is looking at our being. Religion is about *human doings* not *spiritual beings*.

I know firsthand the strangling hold that religion has. I was raised in a religious environment around religious people. I wondered for years why I saw so many church people living defeated lives. This is not a criticism or a judgement; this is what I saw firsthand.

It made me very confused about God, because I saw people singing songs about God being the healer, but they were sick. I saw people testifying about God being their provider, but they were enslaved to poverty. I saw people portray themselves as loving individuals in church, but inwardly they were full of bitterness and resentment. To a young person coming up in church, it sends mixed signals. I understand that culture affects the way we tend to perceive religion, but I want to clarify what I mean by the term *religion*. In short, it is any effort on our part to please God through our performance.

Many people are living frustrated lives because they are rejecting this simple truth—being a Christian is not a religion. The moment we attempt to package Christianity in the box of every other religion, we make it appalling and off-putting. It is like a police officer who takes bribes or a corrupt politician; no one wants that.

Things are only beautiful in life when they are functioning according to their purpose. If you don't believe me, try to fly with no technological aid and you will see quickly that a man is not a bird. We will never be birds. By the same token, Christianity will never be a religion. It was never intended to be!

HE'S ALIVE!

That if thou shalt confess with thy mouth the Lord Jesus, and shalt believe in thine heart that God hath raised him from the dead, thou shalt be saved (Romans 10:9).

The simple truth is that Jesus Christ is alive; He is not dead! We are not just following the sayings of a dead religious leader like most other religions are; we are engaging with the very fullness of the Godhead embodied in the person of Jesus Christ. This living person dwells within us by virtue of the new birth—via the Holy Spirit.

God has made us alive in Christ. Religion, on the other hand, kills people. Please understand that there are positive aspects to every religion, but they are not intended to make anyone alive. This is why when we try to be religious in an attempt to follow Jesus, we enter into a "rat race." In other words, we begin a cycle that we find very difficult to get out of. It becomes a lifestyle of failure and frustration, then more failure.

There are so many people today who are unnecessarily battling depression and defeat because they don't know that Jesus already paid the price. They don't realize that to be a believer means to have the very life of God operating on the inside of them, and that spiritual life is able to affect change in every area of their lives. The Holy Spirit has the power to quicken us (make us alive) and produce a quality of living that we cannot even fathom. Oh, what a mystery!

Sometimes it is hard for us to admit that we are in this place. A place where we are dissatisfied with the results we are getting. A place where going to church is not yielding the results we desire. A place where our attempt to be morally good is not working. A place where we say things like, "God, I will never do it again," yet we find ourselves doing it again and again. Jesus did not come to make us religious; He came to make us alive! The moment we accept this very simple truth, we enter into a new reality. A reality of victory!

PRAYER OF ACTIVATION

Lord Jesus, You are not a list of dos and don'ts, You are God incarnate and You want to walk in covenant relationship with me. I have failed, I have been broken, and I need to be restored. I cannot do any of this in my own strength. Only Your Holy Spirit has the power to bring me to life. Show me where I have made my relationship with You into a religion, and help me release my own pride so that I may fall more deeply in love with You! Amen.

FOR DISCUSSION

1. What does the word *Christian* mean?

2. God wants to awaken a deeper desire for Himself in your generation. If being a believer is not for religious people, who is it for?

3. Invite the Holy Spirit to help you examine your heart and your walk with God. What spiritual practices might have become religious rituals in your life?

LIVING FROM
HIS PRESENCE

I can vividly remember my mother listening to popular gospel songs when I was growing up. There was one particular gospel song that stood out in my mind. The lyrics of the song went as follows: *"I'm coming up on the rough side of the mountain, and I'm doing my best to make it in."* This song was very popular when I was a child. However, I couldn't understand how those lyrics were so well received by Christians. It just seemed so depressing to me. I could not wrap my mind around the idea that we have to suffer for the rest of our lives until we make it into heaven. Even though I wasn't very spiritual at the time, I knew that there was something wrong with that line of thinking. It was not until I gave my heart to the Lord that I realized my assessment was correct.

Many Christians live their entire Christian lives focusing on *"try-ing to make it into heaven."* I know there may be some exceptions to this. However, the point I am making is that for nearly 1,000 years, the Church's entire focus has been *"living to get to heaven,"* when in fact this was never the focus of the New Testament. In the New Testament, the paradigm was not living *for* heaven but living *from* heaven. In Ephesians, the Bible says that we are seated with Him in heavenly places in Christ Jesus (see Eph. 2:6). Colossians 3:1-3 says:

> *Therefore if you have been raised up with Christ, keep seeking the things above, where Christ is, seated at the right hand of God. Set your mind on the things above, not on the things that are on earth. For you have died and your life is hidden with Christ in God* (NASB).

This theology seems to conflict with the antiquated philosophy that we must somehow struggle and strive to try to make it in. On the contrary, God has called every believer to demonstrate our heavenly citizenship in the earth. This is why the apostle Paul said, in the book of Philippians, that our citizenship is in heaven. If you are truly born again, you have citizenship in heaven. Therefore, you ought to live like it. This is the essence of true holiness. We are supposed to live like the people God says we are. There is no bondage in heaven; therefore, we should not be bound on the earth. There is no addiction in heaven; therefore, we should not live in addiction on the earth. There is no immorality in heaven; therefore, we should not live immoral lives on the earth. The key is understanding who we are and where our true citizenship lies.

I travel quite frequently, and as a result I have the opportunity to see and observe many things. Oftentimes when I travel, I am very excited to come back to the United States. When I land on US soil, I never once question whether or not I will be accepted back into the country. Why? Because I am a citizen. Citizenship carries with it particular benefits. As a citizen of the United States, I have the ability to travel the world as a US citizen and return back home. No matter where I go, I am still a US citizen. In essence, I don't just live *in* the United States, but I live *from* the United States. This is the power of citizenship.

In the same manner, we are citizens of heaven. We are not just living *in* heavenly places, but we are living *from* heavenly places. Imagine how this change in perspective can transform our lives. It is not my righteous behavior that causes me to enter heaven, but it is my heavenly positioning that causes me to behave righteously. We cannot earn our way into heaven. The blood of Jesus has provided for that. However, if we are truly born again we should walk worthy of our vocation in God. This is true both morally and spiritually. I want you to ask yourself this question: "What does heaven look like?"

I have great insight into the answer to that question. One reason for that is because I have seen heaven. The very first vision of heaven I ever had was when I first became a believer. In this vision, I saw Jesus sitting on the judgment seat. There were endless numbers of people standing in line to come before Him. He didn't say much. He simply pointed His fingers and people would either enter into joy or they would be cast into darkness. You can imagine that this was a very sobering vision for me.

The second major visitation to heaven involved me standing in a very large courtyard. Across from this courtyard was a throne room. I heard a sound come from the throne room, and once the sound was released oil began to fill the courtyard. It saturated my feet, and then immediately I was back in my body. I can vividly remember the peace and the bliss in heaven. The atmosphere was so pure and holy. There was no darkness or fear, just unconditional love and grace. Once you have a glimpse of what heaven looks like, you have a picture of how God wants you to live on the earth.

DAYS OF HEAVEN ON EARTH

And from the days of John the Baptist until now the kingdom of heaven suffereth violence, and the violent take it by force (Matthew 11:12).

We shared earlier that the presence of God is much more than a feeling or an emotion. The presence of God is the manifest atmosphere of heaven. It is the expression of heaven's environment on the earth. The presence of God is an extension of God's character. The Bible says that in the days of John the Baptist until Christ, the kingdom of heaven suffers violence and the violent take it by force. I like the way the Amplified Bible puts it:

> *From the days of John the Baptist until now the kingdom of heaven suffers violent assault, and violent men seize it by force [as a precious prize].*

Developing a supernatural lifestyle requires both intentionality and audacity. We must make a choice whether we are going to exist until we enter into the sweet by and by or seize heaven as a precious prize. The word for "take" or "seize" is the Greek word *harpazō*, which means to carry off by force, to claim for one's self eagerly, or to snatch away (Strong's G726). In other words, we must appropriate the culture of heaven in the earth realm. This must be done daily! The word used here is the same word from which we derive the Latin word *rapture*. According to God's Word, it is possible to get "caught up" in the presence of God every day.

King David described it this way:

> *He that dwelleth in the secret place of the most High shall abide under the shadow of the Almighty* (Psalm 91:1).

The term *secret place* was a common idioma
chamber. It described a place of intimacy and
where vows between a husband and wife w
presence of God is a place of intimacy and i
deposited within us every time we enter the sec.
that affects every area of our lives. In the Old Testament, a w.
enter into a secret chamber to consummate the marriage with the expectation that she would come out pregnant. In the same way, the presence
of God impregnates us with passion, purpose, and power. You can tell
when a man or woman has been with God. The way they speak, behave,
and look is transformed by the presence.

> Through the Holy Spirit, every
> believer can experience heaven
> on earth.

COURIERS OF THE PRESENCE

One of my first major jobs after high school was working as a courier
for the county, specifically the courts. I was tasked with transporting
very important court documents to the various courts throughout the
county. This included everything from subpoenas to court orders. Each
morning I would load up my van with sealed documents. The courier
bags were locked and only opened upon arrival to their final destina-
tion. Little did I know that God was trying to reveal a very profound
truth to me within my own job description. We are couriers of the presence of God. We have been called to release His presence into the earth.

people will never come into contact with a church building, but will come into contact with God's presence in and through you. The Bible says, *"What? know ye not that your body is the temple of the Holy Ghost which is in you, which ye have of God, and ye are not your own?"* (1 Cor. 6:19).

The Holy Spirit doesn't belong to us, but He resides in us and wants to express Himself through us. I will never forget an instance several years ago when God began to teach me about His presence. I was walking down the promenade of the university I attended at the time. As I walked up the stairs of the library, a young man called out to me and said, "Excuse me, can I pray with you? I sense that you are a man of God, and I just want to pray with you." I reluctantly said yes. Where I am from, it is not normal for people to approach someone else in such a manner. He grabbed my hand and prayed for me. As we were praying, I felt another hand grab mine. It was rough and calloused. I could smell a very pungent odor as the person drew closer. I slowly opened one eye and saw a homeless man praying with us. This was very strange! Once we concluded the prayer, the homeless man said, "I was drawn to the presence around you guys." That homeless man gave his life to Christ that day. Hallelujah! Never underestimate the power of the presence of God.

On another occasion I was in class, and a young lady grabbed me by the hand and led me outside the classroom. In my mind, I was certain she was about to flirt with me, being that I was such a good-looking young man, but on the contrary she asked for prayer. She said, "I don't know you, but something told me I should ask you to pray for me. I am going through a very difficult time right now." Tears welled up in her eyes as she looked at me with a piercing gaze. We never had a single conversation before this moment, yet "something" told her to ask me for prayer. We must be mindful that we carry God's presence everywhere we go. People may not understand dogma or theology, but they can feel the presence of God. To prove this point even further, I'll share another story. I was listening to some worship music on YouTube one night and I noticed that a Muslim woman commented on the video. She stated that though she was a Muslim, there was such a presence on the song that she loved it. Don't get me wrong—nothing replaces the gospel of Jesus Christ, but the gospel of Jesus Christ, when properly embraced, releases a supernatural presence that is undeniable.

THE MYSTERY OF JACOB'S LADDER

The Bible says in Genesis 28:

And Jacob went out from Beersheba, and went toward Haran. And he lighted upon a certain place, and tarried there all night, because the sun was set; and he took of the stones of that place, and put them for his pillows, and lay down in that place to sleep. And he dreamed, and behold a ladder set up on the earth, and the top of it reached to heaven: and behold the angels of God ascending and descending on it. And, behold, the Lord stood above it, and said, I am the Lord God of Abraham thy father, and the God of Isaac: the land whereon thou liest, to thee will I give it, and to thy seed; and thy seed shall be as the dust of the earth, and thou shalt spread abroad to the west, and to the east, and to the north, and to the south: and in thee and in thy seed shall all the families of the earth be blessed. And, behold, I am with thee, and will keep thee in all places whither thou goest, and will bring thee again into this land; for I will not leave thee, until I have done that which I have spoken to thee of. And Jacob awaked out of

his sleep, and he said, Surely the Lord is in this place; and
I knew it not (Genesis 28:10-16).

Hidden within this familiar biblical passage is a secret to living from the presence of God every day. Concealed in the text is a spiritual pattern that, once understood, will take your spiritual life to another dimension. Let me explain!

> In God's kingdom pattern of manifestation, we must first ascend in intercession and worship before we can descend with power and authority.

Jacob traveled toward an area called Haran. Interestingly enough, the word *Haran* means "mountaineer." Jacob was about to have a mountaintop experience. From a biblical perspective, mountains represent a place of ascension and revelation. In other words, what God was going to reveal to Jacob was going to bring him into a greater dimension and deeper revelation. Jacob had a dream in which he saw a ladder set up on the earth, the top of which reached heaven. The next thing that Jacob observed was a company of angels ascending and descending on the ladder. And God stood above it. A few things here are very important to observe. First, the ladder was set up on the earth and reached to heaven. The pattern that we see is ascending and descending. This is a major key. It does not say descending and ascending. Why? The angels Jacob witnessed were actually human beings. That is why they were in the earth. The word *angel* often means messenger and can also refer to human agents.

Without ascending there can be no descending. The word *ascending* here means "to be taken up, to go up, or to be carried away." This is similar to the word used for "caught up." As the saying goes, what goes up must come down. As you and I are intentionally caught up in His presence, we are able to come down with power in the same way that a rock thrown into the air gains velocity and makes a greater impact when it lands than when it left the earth. God wants us to make an impact in the earth. One of the Hebrew words for descending is *yarad*, and one of its meanings is "to march down" (Strong's H3381). After Jacob witnessed the angels ascending and descending, he immediately heard the voice of the Lord speaking and confirming the promise that He would give him the land promised to his fathers. Possession of the land follows the ascending and descending of the angels. There must be an initiation from the earth in order to see manifestation from heaven. This is more than a dream; it is actually a supernatural vision that reveals a heavenly pattern. Those angels were intercessors who had been commissioned to ascend in God's presence and release the power of God. God is looking for a generation of intercessors who will storm the gates of heaven and pull down heavenly resources into the earth.

In verse 17, the Bible says of Jacob, *"And he was afraid, and said, How dreadful is this place! this is none other but the house of God, and this is the gate of heaven."*

The word *gate* here is literally translated "marketplace." A marketplace is defined as an open space where a market is or an area of commercial dealings and trade. It is a place where transactions take place. In other words, the agents of the kingdom of God are ascending into the marketplace of heaven and descending to effect change in the earth. We are God's messengers to this generation. We are His heavenly brokers (those who facilitate exchange). God is calling you to ascend and descend. Every time we ascend in worship and communion with

God, we descend with heavenly power to affect change in the atmosphere around us.

AMBASSADORS OF THE KINGDOM OF GOD

The Scriptures tell us in Second Corinthians 5:20 that we are ambassadors of Christ. An ambassador is someone who represents a kingdom or government in a foreign territory. If you visit the ambassador of China, the décor and the environment of that embassy will resemble China. If you visit the Italian ambassador, there will be a reflection of Italy in his or her office. Why then do we think it would be acceptable for people to come into contact with us and never get a glimpse of what heaven looks like? This is what we as ambassadors have been tasked with.

PRAYER OF ACTIVATION

Lord, teach me to live as a citizen of heaven. I want to be holy, as You are holy, and carry Your presence into the world. Express Your nature through me, I pray. Help me to bring the kingdom of heaven with me as Your ambassador. Amen.

FOR DISCUSSION

1. What two things are required to develop a supernatural lifestyle?

2. Psalm 91:1 says, *"He that dwelleth in the secret place of the most High shall abide under the shadow of the*

Almighty." What happens when we enter the secret place?

3. In God's kingdom pattern of manifestation, before we can descend with power and authority, what must we first do?

CHAPTER 7

SEEING THROUGH HEAVEN'S EYES

Years ago, I was driving from Pensacola, Florida back to Atlanta, Georgia. At that time my father and I would often go fishing, and this was one of my earliest deep-sea fishing trips. While we were traveling on our way back to Georgia, I heard an audible voice speak to me from the clouds. This is what the voice said: "Preach My Word." You can imagine my surprise as a 15-year-old boy hearing these words. Up until this time, this was the most ominous experience I had ever undergone. This was my first supernatural encounter with God. This was the first time I realized that I was called into the ministry. But this encounter also represented something else—God saw me as greater than I saw myself. That experience reminds me of when God spoke to the prophet

Jeremiah and told him that before he was formed in his mother's womb, He (God) knew him. From that moment onward, I began to see myself differently. I realized that there was something greater than the world of which I was aware. There was definitely something beyond my current reality. Why would the Creator of the universe call a little boy with ADHD to preach for Him? Heaven had an agenda for me that was greater than the agenda I had for myself. Though I saw my frailty and my weaknesses, God saw greatness in me.

Believers have no idea how God really sees them. Maybe you're thinking to yourself, "I am just a regular person." *News flash*—there are no "regular" people in the kingdom of God! The Bible says in First Peter 2:9, *"But ye are a chosen generation, a royal priesthood, an holy nation, a peculiar people; that ye should shew forth the praises of him who hath called you out of darkness into his marvellous light."* My friend, there is much more to your life than meets the eye. The key is learning to look at yourself through the correct lenses. Just like I realized this for me, you too must understand and accept that heaven's agenda for you is greater than the one you have for yourself. It's time for you to stop holding back and let *all* heaven break loose!

Let's look at someone who made a terrible mistake but was repentant and therefore restored to his position in God. I am talking about the famous disciple Simon Peter. Can you imagine how Peter felt when he heard the cock crow? Can you picture the shame and embarrassment he experienced as the words of Jesus reverberated in his ears? *"Before the cock crows, you will deny Me three times!"* He was broken and defeated. He realized the depths of his own hypocrisy and frailty. This is the great Peter who promised the Lord he would never deny Him. Who would have thought that the strongest among the apostles would become the weakest in a moment of humanity? Yet even so, heaven had a greater agenda!

After His resurrection, Jesus immediately restored Peter to dignity and purpose, and at the Day of Pentecost it was none other than Peter who stood up and preached to a city. Heaven literally broke loose in the Book of Acts when tongues of fire came down and consumed the believers in the Upper Room. The power of the world to come was manifested simply because someone was willing to see themselves from heaven's perspective. When Jesus restored Peter to an even greater position than he had been before, he was immediately changed. My questions to you are, "How do you see yourself today? Are you just a sinner saved by grace? Or are you an ambassador of Christ?" Don't get me wrong—we should all appreciate the grace of God in salvation, but the greatest way to demonstrate our gratitude to God is by becoming the people, the body of Christ, the body of immovable believers He has called us to be (and sees us to be). One of the most powerful keys to living a supernatural life is seeing through heaven's eyes. What do I mean by "seeing through heaven's eyes"? Great question!

In John 1:48, the future disciple Nathanael asked Jesus an important question. He asked our Lord, *"How do You know me?"* Jesus answered him and said, *"Before Philip called you, when you were under the fig tree, I saw you"* (NASB). The Greek word for "saw" here literally means "to perceive, discern, or examine" (Strong's G1492). In other words, Jesus discerned Nathanael's truest and deepest identity. He recognized who Nathanael really was. This was not an ordinary seeing but a perceiving of value from heaven's perspective. If we are going to live a supernatural life, it is critical for us to understand the way the Father sees us. Nathanael responded to Jesus's answer with, *"By this, I know you are the Son of God! You are the King of Israel!"* (see John 1:49). Nathanael realized that it was actually impossible for Jesus to have physically seen him under the fig tree, because the fig tree was not a few feet down the road within sight from where Jesus was. Yet, he knew that

Jesus had seen him somehow, so he recognized that the exclamation was not based on natural sight at all!

LET ALL HEAVEN BREAK LOOSE

Worship doesn't just change the way we see God; it changes the way we see ourselves. The presence of God alters our vision supernaturally. When we learn to operate in God's presence, we learn to see the world around us from heaven's perspective. Miracles are birthed from miraculous vision. When we learn to see the world around us from heaven's perspective, we can demand that the world around us conform to the image that we see. This was one of the first things that began to change our ministry. Many people ask me how I broke into the supernatural. This breakthrough had everything to do with the way I saw things. When I would encounter sick people, I learned to *see* them healed. When I encountered people who were bound, I learned to *see* them free. When I encountered people who were broken, I learned to *see* them restored.

Your perspective is paramount in releasing the power of God in your life. If you simply see yourself as a rotten sinner, trying but barely making it into heaven, you will cultivate a life of defeat. But if you *see* yourself as someone positioned for victory, you will begin to release God's power in your life in a way you have never experienced. You have probably heard the statement, "Perception is reality." Though this statement is often used as a New Age cliché, it is very, very true. This is why God is constantly confronting the way we see things. He knows that we will ultimately conform to what we see on a constant basis. God is invested in us, and He is concerned about what we see because what you *see* is what you will *seize*—reach out and grab hold of!

The Bible says we are conformed into His image from glory to glory.

MADE IN HIS IMAGE

Most of us know the story of the creation of man found in Genesis chapters 1 and 2, but do we really know the story? The Bible says in Genesis chapter 1 that God said, *"Let us make man in our image, after our likeness"* (Gen. 1:26). Why did God use the word *image*? What is the significance of this terminology? The word *image* there literally means "in the likeness of that which is seen in heaven" (Strong's H6754). In other words, God used Himself as the pattern and the standard with which He created man. Another word for "image" is *likeness* or *facsimile*. A fax is a replica of that which was originally transcribed. Therefore, when God made man it was His intent for the earth realm to be a reflection of the heavenly realm. This does not necessarily mean that man represents the exact physical attributes of God, but it does mean that man represented His moral likeness, His character, and His spiritual dominion. He intended for all of the created world to look at man and see the image of the incorruptible God. The apostle put it this way: *"We are his workmanship"* (Eph. 2:10). The word *workmanship* there literally means "production" or "creation." God literally produced us in His own image and likeness. This means that we are representations or replicas of heaven. You may be thinking, "That just can't be!" But it is true. Religion and tradition have taught us that we have no real value. We are just wretches. The devil is a liar! John 3:16 tells us *"For God so loved the world, that he gave his only begotten Son, that whosoever believeth in him should not perish, but have everlasting life."* If you and I have no value, why would God give the most valuable thing in the universe to redeem us?

The truth is, we are valuable to God because He created us in His image, and God values Himself; therefore, anything made in His image has value. We are His craftsmanship, masterpieces designed by the Master Creator. This is why heaven rejoices every time a sinner comes to repentance. It represents the redemption of something God holds in high esteem. Jesus taught that the kingdom is like a pearl of great price, one so valuable and precious that if it is lost a person will do nearly anything to get it back. What does this have to do with living from His presence on a daily basis? Everything! Because once you realize who you are in Christ, you will be able to appreciate the value of His presence in you.

DOING WHAT WE SEE THE FATHER DO

There is no doubt that Jesus Christ is our highest example of supernatural living. John 14:12 records Jesus stating, *"The works that I do shall he do also; and greater works than these shall he do; because I go unto my Father."* We are empowered by the Holy Spirit to do the works of Jesus and greater. The question is, what were the works of Jesus? Jesus did what he saw the Father doing. Jesus built His earthly ministry on a life of intimacy with the Father whereby He was able to gaze into the Father's heart and see His desires for the people. This is the biblical pattern for New Testament ministry.

Several years ago, the Lord told me that He wanted me to teach and equip His people to walk in the supernatural inheritance. At the time, I didn't really know what this meant. But slowly and surely, the Lord began to increase my desire to see His miraculous power manifest. He showed me in a vision that His people were spiritually in need of suste-nance. As I pressed into this vision, I began to see God's power in ways I had never seen it before. I remember being in a meeting one night, and I began to describe a vision in which the river of living water began to flow and touch everyone in the room. As I continued to describe this vision, I felt the presence of God. It was so strong that the people lis-tening to me began to fall under the power of God. They were literally overwhelmed by God's presence. Months later, we began to see and hear reports of creative miracles. People with metal in their legs testified that the metal had turned to bone. On one occasion, a woman with cancer we were praying for reported to us that the cancer dissipated from her body and the doctor gave her a clean bill of health!

INCREASE IN HEAVENLY ENCOUNTERS

One of the things that began to happen as I became more sensitive to the presence of God was an increase in heavenly visions and a height-ened awareness of angelic activity. In fact, the more I teach on this subject, the more people experience heavenly encounters and/or angelic visitations. For the sake of balance, I want to emphasize the fact that, as believers, we should not live for angelic visitations or worship angels; we worship Jesus, but supernatural experiences are available to every believer and are even encouraged in Scripture. There is no doubt that angels are attracted to the presence of God, and the more we abide in and cultivate the presence of God in our lives, the more angels show up.

My first angelic visitation was over 20 years ago. Up until this point I didn't know that people could have real angelic encounters today. One night while lying in my bed, I felt a presence in the room with me. This was not a frightening presence, but I was aware that I wasn't alone in the room. As I opened my eyes, I saw an angel staring at me with the most perplexing gaze. It was as if he wanted to figure out what all the fuss was about. As I tried to ascertain exactly what was happening, he vanished at what seemed to be the speed of light. As I came out of this encounter, I heard the word *rest*. During that time, I was going through tremendous spiritual warfare. It was then I realized that God sent an angel to minister to me. The Bible refers to angels as ministering spirits. They have a unique assignment to minister to those of us who are heirs of salvation. Notice that when the angel Gabriel appeared to Daniel, he identified himself as Gabriel who stood in the presence of God. These angels behold God's presence day and night. Whenever we create an atmosphere conducive to the presence of God, we create an atmosphere of angelic visitation. And angels never show up empty-handed. There is a third Great Awakening coming to the body of Christ, and it will be marked with signs, wonders, miracles, mass salvations, resurrections, and angelic encounters. The bedrock of this move of the Spirit will be the revelation of the power and necessity of God's presence.

TESTIMONY OF ACTIVATION

I was raised in a Christian home. My parents were greatly involved in ministry, so growing up I knew much about how a Christian should live and behave. I had a family friend teach me about the supernatural at a very young age. So I knew about it, but not many pastors I heard were teaching me how to live out that supernatural lifestyle. It wasn't until my husband and I met and moved across the country to attend Dr. Kynan Bridges's church that God really opened my eyes again to the supernatural in its full glory. It is such a blessing to be taught by such a spirit-led pastor! Not only does he teach you about the supernatural and how to use the gifts God has given to you, he activates you and opens up the door for you to walk in what he has taught. It is truly amazing! I have seen people healed of many ailments, delivered from bondage, and so much more. Dr. Kynan has greatly impacted my life; he has prayed over me and freed me of past bondage, and I couldn't be more grateful!

PRAYER OF ACTIVATION

Lord, conform me more and more into Your image. I want to walk in heavenly encounters with You, increasing from glory to glory. Show me what You are doing every day so that I can do only what I see You doing. Let heaven break loose in my life, I pray. Amen.

FOR DISCUSSION

1. If you are going to live a supernatural life, it is critical for you to understand the way the Father sees you. How does God see you according to First Peter 2:9?

2. Miracles are birthed from miraculous vision. When you learn to see the world around you from heaven's perspective, what can you do?

3. The Bible says in Genesis 1 that God said, *"Let us make man in our image, after our likeness."* Why did God use the word *image*? What is the significance of this terminology?

CHAPTER 8

RELEASING THE
SUPERNATURAL

What if I told you that it was impossible for a born-again believer to obtain a supernatural life? How would you respond to that statement? You would probably be a little perplexed by it. You would probably think, "But I thought that is what this book is all about!" Actually, you would be incorrect! Why? God never told the believer to obtain the supernatural because you already have it. Imagine inheriting millions of dollars from a very wealthy relative. Now imagine that the funds were deposited in your bank account and made available for immediate release. Instead of appropriating the funds accordingly, you continue to struggle, not able to meet your basic financial needs. This would be a tragedy! Why? Because you already have all the finances you need. You don't need to obtain wealth; you need to release and appropriate the wealth that you have already received.

The most miraculous thing that any person can experience is the miracle of salvation. It was at that moment that the Holy Spirit regenerated you and made you a new creation. Through the infilling of the Holy Spirit, we were baptized with supernatural power! (If you have never received the baptism of the Holy Spirit, we will lead you in a prayer in just a moment.) As a result of this, you already have the power and presence of God dwelling within. We were filled with the full inheritance of the kingdom of heaven. You don't need to obtain the supernatural; you need to release it!

The Bible says, *"He that believeth on me...out of his belly shall flow rivers of living water"* (John 7:38). I love the word *rivers* there. It literally means a torrent. A torrent is defined as a strong and fast-moving stream or a sudden, violent outpouring. This means that there is a torrent of supernatural power residing within you. Every time we actively engage the presence of God, we are releasing a torrent of the supernatural in and through us. This is the reason why coming into God's presence is such a gratifying and necessary experience. In fact, I would submit to you that it is the greatest release that any human being can experience on this side of eternity. There is no greater bliss than God's presence.

THE POWER OF HIS PRESENCE

I can remember being in a revival meeting some years ago. I can also remember preparing the sermon that I wanted to preach. I had all of my notes and all of my points highlighted. Yet when I ascended to the platform, something came over me. All of a sudden, my mind went blank. I could not think of anything, even though I had prepared. I didn't know what to say. It is not often that I run out of words to say. The only word I could muster was the word "Hallelujah." I literally said the same word, *hallelujah*, over and over again for a total of what must have been between 50 or 60 times. Then I began to just worship the Lord. Something broke out in the atmosphere. The joy of the Lord started to hit people in their seats. Some were laughing, others were crying. It was one of the most amazing experiences I've ever had. I began to proclaim the message of Jesus. People were healed and delivered, and many surrendered their hearts to the Lord. I didn't have to work for this miracle to happen. I didn't have to execute a formula. I didn't have to rely on emotionalism or religious jargon. I simply placed a demand on the presence of God. I created an atmosphere conducive to Him. This is one of the major keys to walking in power.

> Every time we create an atmosphere conducive to the presence of God, miracles happen!

One day while I was in the kitchen preparing food, God spoke to me. He told me to look at a particular appliance in my home. In fact, it was a brand-new blender. My wife and I like to blend kale and other natural juices. The Lord said, "Kynan, do you see that blender?" Of course I told the Lord yes. The blender was unplugged. The Lord then said to me, "Can that blender work?"

I said, "No." Then the Lord asked me why. I proceeded to give the Lord the obvious answer: "Because it is not plugged in."

The Lord said, "Exactly! This is the condition of many of My children; they are unplugged from My presence."

You see, the presence of God is the power source for the believer. Many people affirm that prayer is the power source for the believer, and they are right. But prayer without the presence is like a river without a current. In fact, prayer releases the presence of God, and it is the presence of God that energizes our prayer lives. Paul affirmed this in the Book of Ephesians when he said, *"Now unto him that is able to do exceeding abundantly above all that we ask or think, according to the power that worketh in us"* (Eph. 3:20). The word *ask* there means supplication. It is another word for prayer. However, Paul goes on to say that what we ask or pray about is energized according to the power that works in us. No prayer, no presence, no power.

When I first became born again in the '90s, I didn't understand this concept. I remember praying for hours and hours and hours every day. It felt like revving an engine. At times, it felt like I was toiling. Even though I was baptized in the Holy Spirit and knew how to pray in tongues, there was still something missing. One day my mentor walked up to me, and through a word of knowledge he said to me, "Stop trying to work your way into God's presence. You are trying to toil into the presence of God." I knew that what he was saying was true. But that was all I knew how to do. I would wake up early in the morning and pray for hours. Now, I still recommend praying for hours a day. But I want to show you a more excellent way. My mentor told me, "Worship your way into His presence." I didn't know anything about worship. But I thought I would give it a try. The next time I went for prayer, I begin to sing and worship the Lord. I began to tell God how wonderful He was. And the more I began to tell God how good He was, the more evident His presence became. It was as if I could feel Him in the room. He was not some distant deity I was making supplication to, but He was a living, breathing Father whose presence was manifest in the room. I began to weep. Then the most interesting thing happened. From the place of awareness, I began to pray. All of a sudden, prayer became easy. It was no longer a chore, and I wasn't toiling anymore. *It was as easy as breathing.*

PRAYER AND THE PRESENCE OF GOD

I want to explore this principle of prayer a bit further. In the book of the apostle James, we are instructed, *"Confess your faults one to another, and pray one for another, that ye may be healed. The effectual fervent prayer of a righteous man availeth much"* (James 5:16). Have you ever wondered why many prayers go unanswered? Have you ever considered why many believers don't seem to get results when they pray? Referring back to my original example, it is like an appliance that is unplugged or an engine without a spark plug. This is the difference between a mechanical prayer life and a supernatural prayer life. The Bible says that the effectual and fervent prayer of the righteous avails much. What does this mean? The word *effectual* comes from the Greek word *energeo,* which literally means energy (Strong's G1754).

Without energy, our prayer lives are not "highly effective." As I mentioned earlier, God's presence energizes our prayer lives. Just like electricity flows through an appliance and gives it the power it needs to operate effectively, the more we learn to cultivate God's presence in our lives, the more we will see supernatural results when we make supplication. The Bible says, *"Delight thyself also in the Lord: and he shall give thee the desires of thine heart"* (Ps. 37:4). How do we delight ourselves in the Lord? There are two ways to accomplish this—spending time in His Word and spending time in His presence. These two things are inseparable. In a healthy marriage, a husband delights in spending quality time with his wife and vice versa; the same principle stands true in our relationship with God. If a husband said he loved and adored his wife but he never spent any time with her, you would probably question his love. I have said before that the greatest gift God can give any person is His presence. It is a precious treasure.

DEVELOPING A SUPERNATURAL CULTURE

In our church in Tampa, Florida, we have developed a very unique culture of the supernatural. It is common for everyone in the church to prophesy, lay hands on the sick, and perform miracles. Why? We have come to realize that the power of God is not centered around a personality but on the person of the Holy Spirit. Notice that I used the term *developed*. The supernatural must be cultivated. Usually it starts out small (with some exceptions), and we must learn to properly steward what God does in and through us. Every risk you take is an opportunity to go deeper and higher in the things of God. The Bible records in Luke 5:4, *"Now when he had left speaking, he said unto Simon, Launch out into the deep, and let down your nets for a draught."* The term *launch out* refers to a ship that goes out to sea. Typically, the greatest catch is not near the shore but in the deeper parts of the ocean. In the same way, the Lord is calling you and me to launch out! Go further than you have gone before. Many believers are not experiencing the supernatural because they are resting upon the shores of their Christian lives. They stay in the safety zone of religion and tradition. However, the greatest miracles are out in the deep.

The greater the risk, the greater the reward!

THE LAW OF SUPPLY AND DEMAND

I remember the old hand well behind my grandmother's house from when I was growing up. In the early days, hand wells were used to fetch water. You had to prime them with water and then pull down the cast iron lever in order to draw the water from the well. The more you pumped, the more water flowed out! This was a simple principle of supply and demand. The greater the demand, the greater the quantity supplied. The same is true in the spiritual realm. The more we place a demand on heaven, the more we compel heaven to supply that which has been demanded. Contrary to popular opinion, God longs for us to place a demand on His power. As we meditate on the Word of God and press into the presence and power of God, we will see supernatural manifestation in our lives. But it is all contingent upon our level of desperation. Someone asked me, "What do you do when you want to see miracles but you have yet to experience the manifestation?" My answer to this person was to press in more. If you wanted to get in shape physically, you wouldn't go to the gym one time and then quit. That would be ridiculous! The same is true spiritually. You don't just ask God to do something and then go on with business as usual. There must be corresponding action. You must begin to change your thinking and thus change your behavior to conform to that which you desire. The Bible tells us in the Book of Ephesians, *"For we are his workmanship, created in Christ Jesus unto good works, which God hath before ordained that we should walk in them"* (Eph. 2:10).

God has ordained that we do good works. Therefore, effort on our part is involved in cultivating the supernatural life. This is not the same as working for our salvation. The word for "works" used here is *ergon,* which means "business or employment" (Strong's G2041). Jesus said that He was about the Father's business. Every business requires investment in terms of time and capital. If we want to be in the business of the supernatural, we must make a quality investment. Our time and energy must be devoted to seeing the type of life that we desire. We must be like the woman with the issue of blood who placed a demand on Jesus, releasing the virtue that brought about her healing. We must be very careful in the western Christian paradigm not to be caught in the vice of comfort and convenience. There is nothing comfortable about a supernatural life. God will lead you to do things that you have never done before and go places you have never gone before. In so doing, the supernatural will become a normal way of life.

THE POWER OF RISK

On a recent trip to Africa, I had the opportunity to preach to thousands during a midweek meeting. Fortunately for me, this church was no stranger to the supernatural. At one point in the service, the Lord told me to release the fire of the Holy Spirit. I stretched my hands out to the congregation under the leading of the Holy Spirit, and the word "Fire!" came out of my mouth. It was risky, because I didn't know if anything would even happen. Then I told the people that the fire was going to fall upon the congregation. At first, nothing happened. Then all of a sudden, I heard screams and wailing from the back of the church. It began moving through the congregation like a brush fire. The altar was flooded with people who were being touched by the presence of God. It was taking a risk and stepping out by the leading of the Holy Spirit that instigated all of this. Your risk might look different from mine, but you must step out nonetheless. I challenge you to pray a very dangerous prayer. Say, "Lord, what do You want to do through me today?" Then I want you to say, "Lord, use me to be someone's supernatural solution." Did you know that you are the miracle someone is waiting for? Step out in faith and take a risk today!

> # Whatever God can do through you, He can do for you.

Never underestimate the power of taking a risk. This simply means that you are willing to do what God tells you to do even if it is uncomfortable. Many of the people in our church go to the local malls and convenience stores and pray for people in the stores. You will be amazed at the type of results they are seeing. Many have reported that they were physically healed; others are surrendering their lives to Christ. None of this would be possible if people were unwilling to take a risk and make themselves available to the Holy Spirit.

SUPERNATURAL BREAKTHROUGH

Hearing the Word of God involves pressing; there is nothing passive about it. His Word is *causal*, not casual. It initiates change; it doesn't stand by uncommitted and unconcerned. God promises in the Book of Isaiah that His Word does not return to Him empty, but that it accomplishes what He sends it out to do. That is why you and I must be intentional about hearing God's Word. When you choose to obey God on your own time and on your own terms, that is called disobedience, and disobedience delays breakthrough. When it comes to God's instruction, even if we don't fully understand why He is telling us to do or say something, your response must be, "Nevertheless, because You have said it, I will do it." Peter said this in the instance mentioned earlier, when Jesus told Him to launch out into the deep and let down his nets for a catch, even though he knew that they had been toiling all night and hadn't caught anything. He obeyed the Lord's instruction immediately, though he wasn't even sure what would happen, if anything at all. Consequently, they brought up so much fish that their nets were tearing apart! Hallelujah! Jesus gave their fishing business the ultimate boost! That was a supernatural breakthrough if there ever was one.

He is ready, fully willing, and most certainly able to do the same thing for you and me today in every situation concerning our lives. The Lord is concerned about every single detail of your life and of my life. How do I know this? Because the Bible says so! The power of God is more capable than the nature of your situation. To be able to live in and from this reality (and yes, this is *reality*), you must anticipate the power and presence of God working in your life.

God desires to manifest Himself to you and through you! Let's go back to the Old Testament for another example of supernatural breakthrough. Are you familiar with the account of the prophet Elisha and the widowed woman in Second Kings 4? The widow's creditors were threatening to take her two sons and make them slaves as payment for her debt. Naturally, this caused her immeasurable agony and distress. She went to the man of God, Elisha, with her situation because she knew that he walked with God and that God worked through him.

> *Elisha said to her, "What shall I do for you? Tell me, what do you have in the house?" And she said, "Your maidservant has nothing in the house except a jar of oil." Then he said, "Go, borrow vessels at large for yourself from all your neighbors, even empty vessels; do not get a few. And you shall go in and shut the door behind you and your sons, and pour out into all these vessels, and you shall set aside what is full." So she went from him and shut the door behind her and her sons; they were bringing the vessels to her and she poured. When the vessels were full, she said to her son, "Bring me another vessel." And he said to her,*

"There is not one vessel more." And the oil stopped. Then she came and told the man of God. And he said, "Go, sell the oil and pay your debt, and you and your sons can live on the rest" (2 Kings 4:2-7 NSAB).

Wow! Can you say overflow and increase? He told her to borrow any empty vessels or containers her neighbors could give—be it bowls, vases, jugs, anything—and not to gather only a few. In other words, "Bring plenty, because you are about to be given plenty!" Now, we don't know whether the woman was aware of what was about to happen with these vessels, but we do know that Elisha knew exactly what he was about to do for her because the Lord gave him a direct instruction. And what did the woman do with Elisha's instructions? She followed them exactly as they had been given, and the windows of heaven were literally opened to her! Where do you think all of that surplus oil came from? It came directly from heaven! Remember, she only had a small jar of oil, and she used it to fill up multiple vessels. This is what is called a creative miracle. More oil was literally being created as she continued to pour, and the oil only stopped flowing when she didn't have anything left to pour it into. The Lord went above and beyond her need (paying off her debt) and provided enough surplus for them to live on. Elisha told her that she *and* her sons would live on the rest. This woman's obedience caused both her and her seed to be blessed.

You see, when you live in the presence of God, those connected to you are affected by your supernatural lifestyle. We live under an open heaven. As a believer, heaven is open to *you*. To receive a supernatural breakthrough, you must be willing to hear supernatural instruction because a supernatural breakthrough requires supernatural obedience. Launch out into the deep! Like Peter did at the Lord's instruction, you must launch out into the deep at the Lord's command. There will never be a time when you launch out and come up empty-handed. It is God's will for you to receive what He has promised you.

TESTIMONY

Apostle Kynan Bridges has an incredible anointing for teaching and activating people in the supernatural ways of God. I remember one teaching in particular, "Developing a Prophetic Lifestyle," that greatly impacted my life and shifted my mindset. Sometimes people think the things of God only belong in the church, but we learned how prophecy can be encouraging to those who aren't in the building yet. We were taught how Holy Spirit can speak to us in many ways as we go about our day and how living in communion with Him is truly a lifestyle. One day my wife and I were running errands, and when we walked in the store I received a word of knowledge that the cashier had back pain. When we checked out, I had to inquire about the prophetic word I had received about her. Sure enough, when I asked her about her back, she confirmed that she was suffering from a pinched nerve. In that moment, I remembered what Apostle Kynan said, "God's not going to reveal unless He plans to heal!" I asked if I could quickly pray for her and she was healed that very instant.

POSSESSING YOUR SUPERNATURAL INHERITANCE

Believing is necessary for seeing in the kingdom. Faith (the substance of things hoped for, the evidence of things not seen) comes by hearing; therefore, what you hear determines what you see. In John

8:56, Jesus told the religious leaders of the day that Abraham *saw* His (Christ's) day and was glad. The Bible tells us that Abraham *believed* God, and it was accounted to him as righteousness (see Gal. 3:6). The Amplified Bible uses the word *credited* in place of *accounted*. Abraham believed God and it was *credited* to him as righteousness.

The term *credit* is used to indicate recognition for a job well done or something of value being added somewhere, whether it be to a bank account or any other account. God added righteousness (a most valuable deposit) to Abraham because of his faith in what God had spoken to him. What the devil does is to try and inhibit your hearing because he knows the power in it.

What you hear affects your paradigm (your perception of the world around you), and your paradigm determines your possibilities. God will sometimes hide manifestation in the message that you hear because He wants you to actively seek Him out. On a regular basis, we must contend to hear God's voice. He has given us the responsibility and the authority to receive what we hear. The choice to use what He has given is entirely yours. Now, you may wonder how you can know whether or not you received a message. For one thing, corresponding action, known simply as *change*, proves that you have received a message. The first thing a message that you receive does is cause you to change your mind; as a result, changes in your attitude begin to take place. When you posture yourself to receive, you are in the proper position to change.

Ask yourself, "Is the Word of God really my final authority?" If so, you will fight for its promises regarding your inheritance as a child of God. Don't base your theology on a gospel song. What does the *Word* actually say about the situation you are facing? What does the Word say about God? If you apply God's Word correctly, you will win every time. Jesus tells us to take heed to what and how we hear. Moving out of position alters the way you hear God. The Lord wants us to be planted so that we can reference His movement. On a regular basis, we should be able to say, "Surely, this is God's doing." *Stand* on what God told you the first time. Taste and see that the Lord is good. God, give us a taste so that we want more! Are you hungry for your inheritance?

> God speaks in the language of opportunities. Opportunities are often invitations to see manifestations of miracles.

You must develop sensitivity to God's Word and Holy Spirit, and you must seize opportunities. What are your reasons for reading the Word of God? Do you read to meet some self-assigned scriptural quota? Or are you searching the Word for hidden treasures? God's living Word, when received, will reverberate in your heart. Allow His Word to saturate your soul. Do you believe that God is good enough to give you your heart's desires? Do you prepare yourself to receive God's message at every opportunity? Are you going to make conscious, deliberate decisions to hear God every day? If so, tell yourself aloud, "I *am* going to hear God today!"

SENSITIVITY TO THE HOLY SPIRIT

When God's people are hungry, something has to happen.

Discouragement interferes with being sensitive to the Holy Spirit. It saps your spiritual energy and keeps you from expecting. Just as a husband develops sensitivity to his wife by spending intimate time with her, you and I can develop sensitivity to the Holy Spirit by being intentional and persistent with the presence of God. Whatever we become sensitive to we become conscious of, and whatever we become conscious of we cultivate. Have you noticed that when people are sensitive to offense or gossip, they are always aware of it? They can find a reason to be offended no matter what. The same is true of the presence of God. When we become sensitive to the Holy Spirit, we begin to feel and discern His presence (or the absence thereof) everywhere we go.

Anticipate the power and presence of God working in your life.

PRAYER OF ACTIVATION

Lord, I worship You with my whole heart today. Help me to plug in to Your presence and step out of my safety zone. Your Word is my final authority, and I know You are good enough to give me the desires of my heart. Lord, what do You want to do through me today? Lord, use me to be someone's supernatural solution. I release what You have already placed within me! Amen.

FOR DISCUSSION

1. How do we delight ourselves in the Lord?

2. How can the term *supply and demand* be applied to the spiritual realm?

3. To receive a supernatural breakthrough, what must you be willing to do?

CHAPTER 9

WALKING IN AUTHORITY

Behold, I give unto you power to tread on serpents
and scorpions, and over all the power of the enemy:
and nothing shall by any means hurt you.

—LUKE 10:19

In the Gospel of Mark, we see a very profound experience unfolding in the lives of the disciples. The Bible says:

> *And after six days Jesus taketh with him Peter, and James,*
> *and John, and leadeth them up into an high mountain*
> *apart by themselves: and he was transfigured before them.*

And his raiment became shining, exceeding white as snow; so as no fuller on earth can white them. And there appeared unto them Elias with Moses: and they were talking with Jesus. And Peter answered and said to Jesus, Master, it is good for us to be here: and let us make three tabernacles; one for thee, and one for Moses, and one for Elias. For he wist not what to say; for they were sore afraid. And there was a cloud that overshadowed them: and a voice came out of the cloud, saying, This is my beloved Son: hear him. And suddenly, when they had looked round about, they saw no man any more, save Jesus only with themselves. And as they came down from the mountain, he charged them that they should tell no man what things they had seen, till the Son of man were risen from the dead (Mark 9:2-9).

Though we have referenced this story before, it is important for the purposes of this book to reference it again. We can say many things about this biblical account, but the thing I want to emphasize is the fact that in this mountaintop experience, God the Father affirmed Jesus and commanded the disciples to "Hear Him!" This is very significant because it deals with authority. There is a direct correlation between God's presence and our authority. In fact, it is in the presence of God that our authority is affirmed. Jesus knew exactly who He was and what He had received from the Father. If we are going to be a people who walk in kingdom authority, we must be a people who know who we are and what we have received from the Father. The next several verses are very important.

And when he came to his disciples, he saw a great multitude about them, and the scribes questioning with them. And straightway all the people, when they beheld him, were greatly amazed, and running to him saluted him. And he asked the scribes, What question ye with them? And one of the multitude answered and said, Master, I have brought unto thee my son, which hath a dumb spirit; and wheresoever he taketh him, he teareth him: and he foameth, and gnasheth with his teeth, and pineth away: and I spake to thy disciples that they should cast him out; and they could not. He answereth him, and saith, O faithless generation, how long shall I be with you? how long shall I suffer you? bring him unto me. And they brought him unto him: and when he saw him, straightway the spirit tare him; and he fell on the ground, and wallowed foaming. And he asked his father, How long is it ago since this came unto him? And he said, Of a child. And ofttimes it hath cast him into the fire, and into the waters, to destroy him: but if thou canst do any thing, have compassion on us, and help us. Jesus said unto him, If thou canst believe, all things are possible to him that believeth. And straightway the father of the child cried out, and said with tears, Lord, I believe; help thou mine unbelief. When Jesus saw that the people came running together, he rebuked the foul spirit, saying unto him, Thou dumb and deaf spirit, I charge thee, come out of him, and enter no more into him. And the spirit cried, and rent him sore, and came out of him: and he was as one dead; insomuch that many said, He is dead. But Jesus took him by the hand, and lifted him up; and he arose (Mark 9:14-27).

Oftentimes when this story is recounted, people tend to focus on the father of the oppressed child, but I want to focus on Jesus. This was a problem that no one else could solve, and yet a man who had been in the presence of God had the answer. We know that Jesus is the Son of God, but this particular miracle is not about the Son of God; it is about the Son of Man. He was not just an example for us but an example of us. What do I mean? In Luke 10, Jesus gave the disciples authority to tread on all the power of the enemy. He had already given them the ability to cast out devils and heal disease, yet they couldn't solve this problem. The Bible makes it clear that Jesus was not happy with this scenario. He said to them, "Faithless and perverse generation." The word *perverse*, as mentioned before, means "twisted." They were under the impression that their authority was temporary and transactional. In other words, it worked when Jesus was around, but when He went up to the mountain, it no longer worked.

How many Christians have authority when the pastor is around, but they become absent-minded when they are dealing with problems in their family or with their finances? The presence of God reminds us of who we are and the authority we possess. In a way, this young oppressed boy represents an afflicted generation waiting for the manifestation of sons who will execute the will of the Father in the earth. Jesus ascended the mountain to have an encounter, but they came down from the mountain to execute authority.

THE AUTHORITY OF THE BELIEVER

I have devoted my entire life to teaching believers who they are and the authority they possess. This revelation transformed my life. For years, I didn't know who I was. I had a passive perception of myself, which was reinforced by a defeated religious mindset. Millions of Christians are being buffeted by a devil they can't even see or identify. Once, I was preaching in a church, and there was a young man in the audience who interrupted my preaching with a loud voice, saying, "What is he talking about?"

The anger of the Lord kindled in me, and I said, "Be quiet you foul devil! Don't say another word!" You could hear a pin drop in the church. There was utter silence.

I went back to my message, and that young man never said another word. After the service, the pastor of the church approached me and asked me if I knew to whom I had spoken. I told him I didn't know. He then proceeded to tell me that this young man was diagnosed with Asperger's syndrome and had a history of outbursts. But when the pastor went to the mother to apologize for the harsh correction during the service, she responded, "Don't apologize! I have never seen my son this peaceful in years. Thank you!"

> When you know who you are, you know what you have the authority to do!

What is the moral of this story? Those were spiritual forces attempting to bring that young man into bondage. Yet God had already given me the authority in Christ to release that young man from his captivity. I will admit that this was not the most polite form of deliverance, but it was effective nonetheless. Many of you reading this right now have experienced the devastation of Satan's bondage. Many of you have cried out in desperation for help and freedom. But you have yet to experience the level of freedom you really desire. I have news for you today—God has given you all the authority that you need to deal with the devil! Why then are so many people in bondage? It's quite simple, actually. They don't know who they are. There is an inextricable connection between the presence of God and our true identity, and there is also a deep connection between our identity and our authority.

The Bible tells us in Romans 8:15 that we have not received a spirit of bondage again to fear, but we have received the Spirit of adoption, and by that truth, we have the right to cry, "Abba, Father." The Spirit of adoption is another name for the Holy Spirit. One of the ministries of the Holy Spirit is to reveal to us our sonship. One of the Spirit's highest, most important assignments is to show you who you really are. God knows that unless you know who you are, you cannot operate in real authority. I'm reminded of the sons of Sceva found in the book of Acts. They were attempting to mimic Paul's ministry of deliverance, and in doing so they spoke to a demon and asked him to leave. To this, the demon responded, *"Jesus I know, and Paul I know, but who are ye?"* (Acts 19:15). Let's just say it didn't end well for those young men.

Why? Because they didn't know Jesus! And without knowing Him, you cannot know who you are. It amazes me how one of the most vital aspects of our Christian experience is often neglected. Many people understand Bible study; we even understand prayer. But do we really understand the absolute necessity of living in God's presence every day? God's presence is not something that replaces the Word or prayer, but it is meant to act in concert with the Word and prayer to bring us into a true revelation of our identity in Christ.

There are churches all over the world led by great Bible scholars, but there is no presence in these churches. If a demon-possessed person can walk into a church and leave demon possessed, then something is terribly wrong. If the sinner can sit during an entire service and not be convicted by the Holy Spirit, then something is terribly wrong. If we can be involved in the church for 20 years and never bring anyone to Christ or never operate in the supernatural, then something is terribly wrong. Understand that my goal is not to criticize or accuse anyone but to provide the solution. God's presence is the solution!

The purpose of my statements is to show us that there is so much more to the Christian experience than what we have accepted. God has called you and me to be people of authority. Let me take a moment to explain authority. What does authority mean? In the Gospel of Luke chapter 9, Jesus gave His disciples authority over all demons and the power to cure all diseases (see Luke 9:1). Interestingly enough, the word for "all" in Greek means *all*. Jesus left no stone unturned as it related to the authority given to the disciples. The word for "authority" there is the Greek word *exousia,* which literally means "the right to act on behalf of another" (Strong's G1849). In other words, God has given us His authority to represent His kingdom in the earth. Why is authority important? Because without authority, we would have no legal jurisdiction over the devil and his demons. Without a badge and a delegation, an officer of the law has no legal right to pursue and arrest criminals. Demons are criminals. Therefore, you and I need authority to deal with them. Just like I dealt with the demon operating through that young man, God has given you the authority to deal with any demon trying to attack you.

I actually do a very in-depth teaching on spiritual warfare and deliverance in which I teach believers how to exercise dominion in their daily lives. The first key to walking in authority is realizing that God is bigger than the devil. As long as you see God and the devil as equals, you will always live a defeated life. But once you recognize that the enemy of your soul is already defeated, you can walk in power and authority in every area of your life.

The presence of God reveals the magnanimity of God's power.

It took me years to really understand and grasp what I am sharing with you in this book. If you are an officer of the kingdom of God and your authority is your badge, then the presence of God is your precinct. Have you ever noticed that police officers report daily to their precinct when they are on duty? That is where they convene daily in order to receive the things they need to exercise the responsibilities of their office. Every day when you wake up, you want to report to the precinct of God's presence to receive the revelation and the insight that you need to conquer your day.

There was a particular woman who began to follow my ministry. Before she heard my teaching on this subject, she was contemplating suicide. Her entire life and family were in chaos. She had come to the end of herself. One day she got a hold of this message. Once she began to put these precepts into practice, her life was radically transformed. She was healed and delivered in a matter of days. Her entire family became radically transformed by the power and presence of God. Now this woman is preaching the gospel of Jesus Christ to everyone around her and walking in victory.

THE TESTIMONY OF MY WIFE

I will never forget the day I met my wife. Apart from salvation, it was the best day of my life. My wife is very tall, and I remember seeing her from afar at a Christian camp. She was serving food as one of the volunteers. I immediately asked the person sitting next to me, "Who is that?"

They replied, "Oh, that's Gloria!" I believe it was love at first sight; the rest, as they say, was history. When my wife and I began courting, she narrated a very vivid dream to me in which many men were trying to lead her. Then I appeared out of nowhere and gently led her to the altar. She was wearing a wedding dress. In her dream, I was at least eight feet tall. Height is very important in a dream; it often signifies spiritual stature or authority. I didn't realize it then, but God was revealing to my wife my stature in the Spirit. Each one of us has a spiritual stature that represents our level of authority. Eight is the number of new beginnings. Nonetheless, it took me some time to grow into the person who would ultimately lead her in life and ministry.

Your spiritual stature is more important than your physical stature.

The point I want to make in sharing this dream is that when I met my wife, she was shy and timid. She never wanted to be seen or noticed and would have been totally content in the background. But deep within, she was a lioness waiting to be unleashed. As I began to teach and minister to my wife, she began to grow in her spiritual authority. On one occasion, she went to a women's conference, and as the guest speakers were ministering the Lord opened my wife's spiritual eyes and she saw what looked like a spotlight in the middle of the floor. The Lord told her to step into it. So she did just that, and the power of God hit her like never before. She wept continually. She was never the same after that experience. Now my wife is a lioness in the kingdom of God. She ministers to women of all ages. And more importantly, she is my greatest partner in life and ministry.

WARRIORS ARISE

Like my wife, God is calling you to rise to the calling and assignment He has given you. He wants you to walk in the authority of Christ. Now is the time for you to be the person He has ordained you to be. Heaven is awaiting your response. Will you answer the call? It doesn't matter where you are today. If you would answer the truth that you are a child of the Most High God and that He has given you His authority, the demons that have been hiding in your life will run for the hills once you walk in biblical authority.

Growing up in the African-American church tradition, you often heard the phrase, "Won't He do it!" That is simply urban vernacular for "God is amazing!" and "He has done it again!" We can all relate to this concept. How many times have you seen God turn an impossible situation around? How many instances has God shown up at the very last minute, when you thought all hope was lost? However, the truth is, the phrase "Won't He do it!" is not an accurate reflection of the heart of God. He is asking us, "Why won't you do it?"

Before you begin to wonder if I am blaspheming, allow me to explain and you'll understand what I mean. How often do you see the chief of police issuing traffic tickets? How many times have you seen the police commissioner directing traffic? Even though they are fully able to do those things, it is not their job to do them. In the same way, why should God do the work He has given us the authority to do? It is our responsibility to exercise the authority He has given us. If the devil is attacking you, take authority over him. It is just that simple, unless you are unaware of your authority or are afraid.

HINDRANCES TO AUTHORITY

Even though the Lord has given us His authority to carry out His will in the earth, we know that there are hindrances to authority. By hindrances, I simply mean things that can infringe on our ability to take authority over the enemy. One of those things is fear! We know from Scripture that the enemy thrives in an environment of fear. Job said, *"The thing which I greatly feared is come upon me"* (Job 3:25). This passage shows us that fear can be a self-fulfilling prophecy. The more we fear something, the less we are able to exercise authority over it. Many Christians treat the devil like he is the Boogey Man; they even speak quietly when they talk about him, as if he will hear what they are saying and retaliate. You would be surprised at how many requests I get from people telling me to pray for them because the devil is after them and their families. The truth is, he will chase after you until you chase him off! Demons are like roaches; they are not supposed to be in your home, but they will stay there as long as you tolerate them. Stop tolerating the devil!

> Whatever you refuse to take dominion over will ultimately take dominion over you.

Another hindrance to authority is willful sin. When believers are operating in continuous and willful sin, they open themselves to the intimidation and oppression of the enemy. Can you imagine allowing someone to live in your house for two years without paying rent, adding their name to the lease, and then asking them to leave? You would be met with resistance simply because you accommodated the person you are asking to leave for so long that they believe they have a right to live in the house. That is what willful sin is like. It is like signing a cohabitation agreement with the devil and then suddenly asking him to leave. The key to breaking this vicious cycle of eviction and reoccupation is true repentance. I am not talking about groveling and begging God for forgiveness, but I am talking about a real change of mind based on the Word of God that produces a change in actions. In Matthew 3, John the Baptist reprimanded the Pharisees who came to be baptized by him, because he knew they were not truly sorry for their sins and only showed up to participate in another activity to be noticed by the people. He sternly rebuked them, demanding that they produce the fruit that shows true repentance. I want to tell you a very powerful secret—the devil can only do what you allow him to do. Nothing more, and nothing less.

> True repentance robs the devil of his legal authority to torment and oppress you.

The third hindrance to spiritual authority is ignorance. The Bible tells us in the book of Ephesians 6:

> *Finally, my brethren, be strong in the Lord, and in the power of his might. Put on the whole armour of God, that ye may be able to stand against the wiles of the devil. For we wrestle not against flesh and blood, but against principalities, against powers, against the rulers of the darkness of this world, against spiritual wickedness in high places* (Ephesians 6:10-12).

You need to know and understand who and what you are fighting (hint: it's not people). I want to draw your attention to the phrase *"rulers of the darkness of this world."* The word *darkness* is the Greek word *skotos*, which means "ignorance or spiritual blindness" (Strong's G4655). Satan and his demons rule in the territory called ignorance. There, he has legal jurisdiction to attack, torment, and oppress believers. What do I mean "legal jurisdiction"? Ignorance is the domain of the devil. The Bible says, *"My people are destroyed for lack of knowledge"* (Hos. 4:6). God said that His people are destroyed as a result of ignorance. What you don't know can hurt you! On the other hand, what you do know can help you. Imagine if someone was ignorant of the law of gravity and they walked off of a ledge; people would be attending their funeral. Why? They were hurt by what they didn't know. Satan thrives off of ignorance because he knows that it rules the darkness. More importantly, you must know who you are in the fight. The people of God do not walk in darkness; as the Scriptures point out, we have been transferred out of darkness into His marvelous light. As a child of God, a soldier in His army, you are already standing in the place of victory. You don't fight from the ground up; you fight from heaven down. You're not fighting to defeat the devil, because the devil is already defeated! You are fighting to establish what God has already spoken. Enforce the will of God in your life and your life will change!

PRAYER OF ACTIVATION

Lord, today I report for duty in the precinct of Your presence. Reveal to me my spiritual stature and give me the revelation and insight to conquer my day. I rise to the calling and assignment You have given me. I answer the call to be the person You have ordained me to be, and I take dominion over the spiritual opposition coming against me. The devil has no authority over me! Amen.

FOR DISCUSSION

1. What is the correlation between God's presence and our authority?

2. One of the ministries of the Holy Spirit is to reveal to us our sonship. It is the highest agenda of having to show you who you really are. Why is this important?

3. God has given us His authority, to represent His kingdom in the earth. Why is authority important?

CHAPTER 10

HIS POWER IN YOU!

Now unto him that is able to do exceeding
abundantly above all that we ask or think,
according to the power that worketh in us.
—EPHESIANS 3:20

What if I told you that you were more powerful than you could ever imagine? What if I told you that the kingdom of darkness was terrified of you discovering what really lies within you? Jesus told the disciples that they should wait to receive "power" before they left Jerusalem. The Bible records in the Book of Acts, *"But ye shall receive power, after that the Holy Ghost is come upon you: and ye shall be witnesses unto me both in Jerusalem, and in all Judaea, and in Samaria, and unto the uttermost part of the earth"* (Acts 1:8).

The word *power* here is very interesting. It is not the same word translated as "power" in Luke 10:19, which refers to authority. The disciples had already been given authority, but they had yet to be given *power*. Power in Acts 1:8 is the Greek word *dunamis*. It literally means "inherent power; the power residing in a thing by virtue of its nature; power for performing miracles" (Strong's G1411). Another concept of the word *dunamis* is explosive power or power that is dynamic in its working. This is where we derive the word *dynamite*. All of the power necessary to produce an explosion is packed within the stick of dynamite. On the outside, it may seem like a simple object, but once ignited—*boom!* In other words, Jesus told the disciples to wait to receive the dynamite. What is the dynamite? It is the explosive power of the Holy Spirit residing within the New Testament believer. This power is supernatural!

The United States military developed an arsenal that is referred to as the Mother of All Bombs or M.O.A.B. It is recognized as the most powerful non-nuclear bomb known to man. This bomb is powerful enough to level a small city. Besides that, the United States has very technologically advanced nuclear bombs that can destroy entire countries. The devil knows that what is in you can level his kingdom. Therefore, he attempts to keep believers ignorant of what they possess on the inside. Why did Jesus tell His disciples to wait for the promise? Because without power, they would not have the ability to be witnesses. To witness means to testify to what you have seen. In order for us to properly represent the kingdom of God and execute the authority He has given us, we must have power. It is like a country that has great authority—without the nuclear power to back that authority, many countries would attempt to encroach upon that nation's sovereignty. The devil may be trying to encroach upon your territory, but you need to pull out the big guns (or in this case, the big bombs) and show him what you are working with.

THE INDWELLING PRESENCE

As we mentioned earlier, God has filled us with His indwelling presence. This presence is the secret to releasing the power of God in our lives. In fact, the Holy Spirit is the most powerful and important person on earth. What do I mean by this? Jesus put it this way: *"But when the Comforter is come, whom I will send unto you from the Father, even the Spirit of truth, which proceedeth from the Father, he shall testify of me"* (John 15:26).

The Holy Spirit is referred to as the "Comforter" and is the Spirit of Truth (the Spirit of Jesus) whom Jesus sent from the Father to live and abide in us. You literally have heaven on the inside. This is why the Holy Spirit is the most important person on the earth—because He reveals Jesus to every believer and brings glory to the Father. The person of the Holy Spirit on the inside of us is the power source of the believer. We have a nuclear dynamo in our spirit that, once released, produces miracle power. The same Spirit that raised Jesus from the dead dwells on the inside of us (see Rom. 8:11). The more we become conscious of this presence, the more we will actively experience the power of God in our lives. I say again, the same Spirit that raised Jesus from the dead dwells within you. Hell and the grave were no match for this power. What an honor! God has chosen broken vessels of clay to fill with His very essence. This is why the Bible says, *"As he is, so are we in this world"* (1 John 4:17). God has placed His presence within us so that we can show the world who He is. You are heaven's marketing plan.

PRACTICING THE PRESENCE

Three centuries ago, there was a man named Brother Lawrence who introduced the Church to the concept of practicing God's presence. He was known for spending hours in the presence of God every day. I believe that the Lord is calling the Church back to a place of intentionally practicing God's presence daily. Most believers conceive of God's presence as something that is attached to a cathedral or a church building. This is why we say things like, "God was in the building!" or "His presence was in that place!" Truthfully speaking, His presence was just as much outside of the building as it was in the building, or at least it should be. Technically, if you are born again His presence is always with you. God is omnipresent, meaning He is everywhere. However, God is very strategic about where His presence abides. Even though He is in every place, He doesn't abide (or rest) upon every place. In the same way, God is in every believer, but He does not rest with and upon every believer. His presence abides where it is welcomed and properly stewarded. When we talk about practicing the presence, we are talking about consciously engaging God's presence on a regular basis.

> Every believer can live in the reality of God's presence 24 hours a day, every day!

In order to do this, we must walk a fine line between awareness and familiarity. We want to develop a sensitivity that makes us constantly aware, but we don't want to become familiar to the point where we take His presence for granted (if it is possible to do such a thing) because familiarity often breeds contempt.

LIVING EPISTLES OF HIS PRESENCE

The Bible says, *"Ye are our epistle written in our hearts, known and read of all men"* (2 Cor. 3:2). In other words, we are living epistles of His presence. We are the letter that the world will read in order to get a deeper understanding of the Father. In this age of email and text messages, it may be hard to comprehend the significance of a letter, but back in the Bible days and even not as long ago as you may think, it was the primary means of communication. Kings and magistrates would send letters to individuals and communities outlining their commands and intentions. They would usually seal the letter with a signet ring to signify the authority and identity of the one sending it. Without the seal, the letter had no legal authority. When God wanted to send His message of salvation to the earth, He sent His only begotten Son. When God wanted to send His message of the gospel of Jesus Christ, He sent His sons (plural). We are His letter to this generation. This is why the Bible says that we have been "sealed" with the Holy Spirit of promise (see Eph. 4:30). This is why we must not grieve the Holy Spirit, because He is our seal. Once a seal is broken or damaged, the letter has no more merit. The letter has no power! Without the Holy Spirit, we have no power and would be unable to have influence in the earth.

> The Holy Spirit validates our witness and gives our message authenticity and power.

The word *influence* is derived from the Latin word *influentia* (where we also get *influenza*, or "the flu" for short). Ancient astrologers believed that there were certain individuals who possessed ethereal fluid in their veins. They were believed to be the children of the stars. These individuals were said to possess *influentia* or the supernatural ability to affect the thinking of others. In other words, they were people of influence.

I know that this is a New Age concept, but they stole it from the Bible. You and I have been born from above, and we are not ordinary beings anymore. I am reminded of Moses who, when he was in the mountain with God for 40 days and nights, had a radical encounter with the presence of God. When he descended from the mountain, the Bible says that his faced shone so bright with the glory of God that the people were not able to behold his face. Here we can see that something happened to Moses in the mountain. This encounter with God affected him in a tangible way. What was imparted to him in the mountain affected everyone around him when he came down from the mountain. This is how influence works. When we have been with God in the mountain, we have influence in the valley. These encounters are designed to reveal to people "The God of the Mountain." Hallelujah!

TRANSFORMED IN THE MOUNTAIN

One day someone made an interesting comment to me. They said to me, "Your face is shining." I thought that maybe I had put on too much lotion and looked greasy or something. But before I could ask for clarification, they said, "I can tell you have been with God." Is this really true? Can people really tell when and if we have been with God? I believe the answer is yes! Compare it to this: can people tell when you've been in the shower? Can people tell when you've been to the gym? The answer to both of these questions is yes. Why? Both of these activities affect the way you look and the way you smell. What if I told you that God's presence has an aroma? It is like spraying perfume on your body. Even after you initially sprayed the perfume, there is a residue that affects everyone around you. In the same way, God's presence affects us all day long. Not only does it affect us, but it affects the people around us.

To give you another example, I will refer to a husband and wife. Can you imagine a husband and wife getting into an argument right before they go to church? No matter how calm the husband attempts to be, the wife's demeanor will reveal that they have been in an argument. Human beings are naturally impressionable. Why? We were created to be impressed by God's presence. Who, what, and how we worship affects everything in our lives. I often tell the worship team at my church that the people in the congregation will always be able to tell whether or not they have spent time with God. I encourage them to never stand before the people unprepared.

THE POWER OF NOW

One of the most critical keys to releasing God's presence and operating in the supernatural is understanding the power of now. What do I mean by *the power of now*? The Bible says in Hebrews 11:1, *"Now faith is the substance of things hoped for, the evidence of things not seen."* It is important to understand that God lives in the realm called "now." *Faith* operates in the now. The term simply means "at the present time or moment." We will deal with this concept a little later, but it would suffice to say that eternity is not the future. In the book of John, Jesus met a woman at a well in Samaria. This woman was asked by our Lord to fetch a bucket of water. The woman responded, *"How is it that thou, being a Jew, askest drink of me, which am a woman of Samaria? for the Jews have no dealings with the Samaritans"* (John 4:9). She had a preconceived notion of who Jesus was and who she was, for that matter. The Scripture says, *"Jesus answered and said unto her, If thou knewest the gift of God, and who it is that saith to thee, Give me to drink; thou wouldest have asked of him, and he would have given thee living water"* (John 4:10). Most of us know the rest of the story; Jesus confronted her immoral lifestyle and revealed that He was not your average Jewish rabbi. Then He made a most profound statement:

> *Jesus saith unto her, Woman, believe me, the hour cometh, when ye shall neither in this mountain, nor yet at Jerusalem, worship the Father. Ye worship ye know not what: we know what we worship: for salvation is of the Jews. But the hour cometh, and now is, when the true worshippers shall worship the Father in spirit and in truth: for the Father seeketh such to worship him. God is a Spirit: and they that worship him must worship him in spirit and in truth* (John 4:21-24).

This Samaritan woman had no idea that what she anticipated as something coming in the distant future was staring her in the eyes. *"God is a Spirit: and they that worship him must worship him in spirit and in truth."* What does this mean? It means that those who worship Him must know who He is and how He operates. God dwells in the now, and this is why we must worship Him now. Most Christians see worship as an event and are unaware that true worship is a lifestyle of constant engagement with the eternal realm. Many people are constantly focusing on what God is *going* to do, what He is *going* to say, and what they are *going* to encounter. However, true worship recognizes that God is always in the now.

Everything that God is doing in our lives it is in the context of eternity—not the past or the future, but in the *now!*

Because many people have the mindset that God is going to do something or going to be somewhere in the future, they never receive what He has already done. Others are constantly dwelling in the past and referencing what God did in ages gone by. This is why many people either talk about the revival that happened 20 or 30 years ago or hope for a revival to hit one day soon. Revival is now because the Spirit of God is now. The key to experiencing revival is engaging His presence *now!* The Spirit of the Lord is here, and He is longing to touch you and transform your life.

The reason why worship is so powerful is because it takes you into the now!

The more you obsess about the future, the more you neglect the power of now. This revelation changed my life. I used to always say, "God is going to use me!" It was like chasing the pot of gold at the end of the rainbow. The more I chased after it, the more it eluded me. Once I realized that God wanted to engage me right where I was, my life changed forever.

PURSUING HIS PRESENCE IN THE NOW

What if I told you that everything you need and desire is in the presence of God? How would you respond to God's presence? I must admit, there was a time in my life when I thought worship was just a part of a church service that prepared people to receive the Word of God. Many times I would come to service right before the preacher began to preach. In my mind, I was skipping the appetizers and going straight for the entree. Little did I know that I was developing a habit of marginalizing God's presence. The truth is, worship (in a corporate sense) is our opportunity to express our devotion and adoration toward God. I would hope that we don't intend to be late for worship service in heaven. That wouldn't be possible anyhow, because our entire existence in heaven will consist of continual worship of the Lamb. If worshiping God bores you now, you probably won't fare too well in heaven.

Every moment in God's presence is a moment of change and transformation.

God is inviting us to encounter His presence in a way that will radically transform our mind, and thus transform our lives. Living in the presence is not an elusive philosophical concept; it is a very practical way of life. If you are experiencing spiritual frustration or spiritual hunger, it is because God is calling you to encounter more of Him. You are heaven's most effective marketing plan. God desires to use you as a vessel of honor to demonstrate how good He really is. Heaven is real; now is the time to prove it!

Prayer of Activation

Lord, I long to live in the reality of Your presence 24 hours a day, every day! I come into Your presence here, on the mountain, so that I will have influence in the valley. Holy Spirit, validate my witness and give my message authenticity and power. Bring me into Your eternal now. Let me be transformed by every moment in Your presence, Lord! Amen.

For Discussion

1. What is the highest agenda of the Holy Spirit and why?

2. What is the first key to walking in spiritual authority?

3. What are three hindrances to spiritual authority and how do you overcome them?

CHAPTER 11

NO MORE FEAR

There is no fear in love; but perfect love
casteth out fear: because fear hath torment.
He that feareth is not made perfect in love.
—1 JOHN 4:18

In everything I have shared, one of the most foundational truths is the truth that God loves you. In fact, God loves you more than you could ever fathom or comprehend. The beauty of God's presence is that it is an expression of His unconditional love for His children. It is a confirmation that He is with us all the time. Did you really hear that statement?

Jesus said, *"I will never leave you or forsake you"* (see Heb. 13:5). How can He make such a promise? He can make this statement because He has given us His presence via the Holy Spirit. Earlier, we said that fear was a hindrance to walking in our authority as believers. Why? Authority is all about confidence and assurance. The more confidence we have, the more powerful we become.

The first thing fear attacks is our confidence in God. Fear is not only a hindrance to the authority of God, but it is a hindrance to us experiencing and enjoying the presence of God. One day, God gave me a very powerful analogy. He said to me, "Kynan, what do your children do when you come home?"

"They run to the door," I answered. "Actually, the moment they hear me outside, they run with anticipation."

Then God asked me, "Why?"

"Because they love me and expect me to bring something good for them."

God began to explain to me that the same is true of our worship and devotion. You cannot separate God's presence from His person (or His character). Every time God manifests Himself, it is an expression of His very nature. My children respond to my presence because they are familiar with my person. If we don't believe and know that God is good, we will be reluctant to approach Him. And as a result, we will ultimately miss out on what He has for us. God never shows up empty-handed.

Fear distorts our perception of things, including our perception of the nature of God. There is a difference between fear (in a threatening or terroristic sense) and reverence. When the Bible speaks of the fear of the Lord, it is talking about honoring and reverencing God out of appreciation and respect for who He is. We respect things when we know what they are and what they can do, but we fear things when we don't know or understand what they are. Essentially, fear is rooted in ignorance. When we are ignorant of a thing, we don't know how to interact with it. For example, many people don't know how to swim because they are ignorant of the nature of water. Because they fear water, they cannot successfully interact with water to accomplish a specific purpose. Many believers are struggling because they have yet to understand or receive the living water.

> God is the eternal Giver of good gifts. He wants to show you how good He is!

THE POWER OF KNOWING

Everything in the kingdom of God is based upon revelation. You must understand that God is so magnanimous and marvelous that the only way we as finite beings can know Him is if He reveals Himself to us. Jesus said in John 17:3, *"And this is life eternal, that they might know thee the only true God, and Jesus Christ, whom thou hast sent."* The word *know* here is *ginosko,* which means "experiential or revelation knowledge" (Strong's G1097). The key to supernatural living is knowing the Father. You cannot know Him and not be impacted by Him and deeply in love with Him. This revelation changes us. It causes us to worship differently, to interact with others differently, and to operate in the world differently. One of the first sermons I remember preaching as a pastor was a sermon entitled "Knowing God." It has always been my conviction that the highest pursuit of every believer is to truly know the Father. The more we know Him, the greater our desire to approach Him. Fear is dissipated in the atmosphere of the knowledge of God.

Many times when we use the term *knowledge*, people assume that we are talking about mental assent, but we are not. Obtaining information is not the same as receiving knowledge. Earlier, we mentioned that knowledge (biblically speaking) is revelatory. I want you to look at it this way—what you know changes what you speak and do now. If there is no change in your thought process and your actions, you have not received knowledge. Notice that within the word *knowledge* is the word *now*. If it does not affect you now, it's not revelatory knowledge. When the Lord truly revealed to me that healing was the children's bread and that we were already healed 2,000 years ago, it transformed the way I prayed for healing and deliverance. It also caused me to get different results. This is why you cannot spend significant time in the presence of God and continue to think and act the same way before you entered His presence.

LET US COME BOLDLY

The Bible tells us in Hebrews 4:16, *"Let us therefore come boldly unto the throne of grace."* The word *boldly* comes from the combination of two Greek words—*meta* and *parresia*. The word *meta* means "behind or after" (in reference to proximity and position), and the word *parresia* means "freedom in speaking, unreservedness, or free and fearless confidence" (Strong's G3326, G3954). In other words, the writer of Hebrews is admonishing us to come close to God without fear or reservation. It is to draw near to God and confidently speak what is on our hearts. Ironically, this is antithetical to many of our religious traditions.

My father was a very strong disciplinarian, so I was often corrected when I did something wrong. The correction often outweighed the affirmation. I was taught (either explicitly or implicitly), as maybe you were, to distance myself from God. I saw God as this impersonal deity far off in the heavens who could not be touched or spoken to. After all, He is someone who waits for the chance to chastise us when we make mistakes, right? This was especially true when there was sin in my life. The sinful nature is inherently distant from God. It is a function of the curse. Because of my perception of God, I found it difficult to approach Him without the sense of fear or shame. I was self-centered in my approach to the things of God. This is why we as Christians are given a new nature through Jesus Christ. As a result, God has called us to come close. In fact, He desires intimacy and proximity with us. He wants us to come so close to Him that we can hear His heartbeat. That's right! His heart is beating with the rhythm of grace and love. In the book of Genesis, God walked with Adam in the cool of the day. This represents the close fellowship He always intended to have with us. He wants to walk with us throughout our daily lives.

Fear encroaches upon our ability to come before God's presence with the full assurance of faith knowing that we are accepted in Him through the blood of Jesus Christ. People are afraid because they often mischaracterize God. These mischaracterizations along with feelings of being unworthy cause people to stay away from God. The Bible tells us that when Adam and Eve fell in Garden, they hid themselves from God's presence. Why? The knowledge of good and evil overshadowed their awareness of God's presence.

And they heard the voice of the Lord God walking in the garden in the cool of the day: and Adam and his wife hid themselves from the presence of the Lord God amongst the trees of the garden (Genesis 3:8).

Many believers are hiding from God's presence. What do I mean by this? The Hebrew word for hid is *chaba'*, which means "to withdraw or to draw back" (Strong's H2244). To withdraw means to remove or leave from a particular place or position. Adam and Eve withdrew themselves from God's presence as a result of sin. Many people today lack the assurance to approach God and enjoy His presence because of sin. Sin produces self-consciousness, which in turn causes self-righteousness or a dependence upon ourselves in the place of God.

This is why it is so important for us to understand the power of righteousness (or right standing with God). Christ's righteousness grants us the confidence to enter God's presence knowing that His presence is the greatest position a believer can stand in. If sin has moved you out of position, repent and get back to the place you belong; you belong in His presence. The Father desires intimacy with you.

GOD WANTS TO BE KNOWN

The simple truth of the matter is that God wants to be known by us. As a matter of fact, He takes pleasure in revealing Himself to us. One of the biggest problems in the Church today is a faulty theology about God. We often portray Him as an old man on a rocking chair in heaven, waiting to "smite" us when we do wrong. But nothing could be further from the truth.

While it is true that God is holy and just, He is also omnibenevolent, and it is the goodness of God that brings out the best in us. If you are going to remove the shackles of fear, you must know who God really is. To whom do we lift our hands in worship? To whom do we sing? With whom do we fellowship? If you cannot answer these questions clearly, then it will be impossible for you to worship God the way He desires. God desires a people who will worship Him in Spirit and in truth.

The Bible says, *"This then is the message which we have heard of him, and declare unto you, that God is light, and in him is no darkness at all"*

(1 John 1:5). When the Bible speaks of light, it is speaking metaphorically of truth, knowledge, and spiritual purity. This means that God surrounds Himself with an atmosphere of revelation. I have said before that the hallmark of heaven is revelation. When we get to heaven we will be in a state of continual awe and astonishment at the eternal revelation of God. Revelation, as we mentioned previously, is simply the unveiling of truth. It is to bring into the light that which was once concealed.

> ## What the devil wants to conceal, God wants to reveal.

We stated earlier that fear is rooted in ignorance. The inverse must be true—confidence and boldness are rooted in knowledge. As the old adage goes, "Knowledge is power!" The more we know God, the more we are able to connect with Him and access His power. The devil disempowers people through ignorance while God empowers people through knowledge. Actually, revelation knowledge increases the flow of God's grace in our lives. The more we know Him, the more we experience Him. The Bible says:

> *Grace and peace be multiplied unto you through the knowledge of God, and of Jesus our Lord* (2 Peter 1:2).

The word *knowledge* here implies correct knowledge. Essentially, as we obtain the proper knowledge of who God is and how His kingdom operates, we begin to experience His grace (favor and power) in ever-increasing measure. The more we come to know God, the more of His goodness we will enjoy. I want you to change your perception of God's presence by changing your perception of God. He is not against you;

He is for you. When you and I come to the realization that we belong in His presence just as much as a bird belongs in the air and the fish belongs in the sea, our lives will take on a brand-new meaning.

THE POWER OF YIELDING

Many years ago, I was invited to a special service on a Sunday evening by a friend. This was referred to as an "anointing service." I was a new believer at the time, and the concept of the "anointing" was very foreign to me. As I sat in the service, I watched the pastor call people forward to pray. I noticed that when he laid his hands on each person they would fall to the ground. This was very strange and offensive. I thought to myself, "Why would they allow themselves to be pushed to the floor like that?"

At that very moment I said to myself, "He will never push me down!" The next thing I knew, the pastor pointed at me and asked me to come forward. I didn't want to cause a scene, so I walked forward to where the pastor was standing. Before I could get within two feet of the pastor, I immediately fell out under the power of God. The ushers literally had to drag me back to my seat. Eventually, I came back to myself and looked around as the service continued. I was so embarrassed! How could I have been so weak-minded? How could I have not resisted?

Even though I was asking all of these questions in my mind, I couldn't deny the overwhelming peace and freedom that I felt when I went out under the power of God. Something happened to me! I literally had an encounter with the Holy Spirit. It was then that I learned a very valuable lesson about yielding to the Holy Spirit. God places a very high value on humility and yielding. These two things go hand in hand. Yet there are many Christians who have yet to truly yield to the Holy Spirit. Why? Quite simply, they are afraid. There is a level of control that we must give up in order for God to do in and with us what He desires. What would happen if we yielded to God the same way we yield to our fears? We would experience God's supernatural power in its fullness.

> Yielding is the act of letting go of control and allowing God to have His way.

Some people have been hurt, wounded, and abused and may find it difficult to yield, but the truth is that the more you surrender to God, the more freedom you will experience. This revelation changed my life. I realized that the fear of losing control was an illusion that the enemy used to manipulate me.

Many pastors are not seeing revival because of the fear of the loss of control. They know that revival and awakening can be unpredictable and they are afraid of what might take place if they let go. I know this is true because I was one of those pastors. One day God spoke to me and said, "Let go!"

I didn't know what the Lord was saying to me until He revealed that I wanted to stay within the safety zone of what I knew and that as a result I was quenching the move of the Holy Spirit. Once I let go of that fear, the Holy Spirit began to manifest Himself in ways we never even imagined. Miracles began to happen. Is the Holy Spirit invited to your church? Is He allowed to change your program? Until God is given the freedom to do what He wants with us, we will never know what it is like to live a miraculous life.

THE SPIRIT OF FAITH

The most powerful remedy for fear is the spirit of faith. The Bible says, *"We having the same spirit of faith, according as it is written, I believed, and therefore have I spoken; we also believe, and therefore speak"* (2 Cor. 4:13). What is the spirit of faith? The Bible tells us that faith is the substance of things hoped for and the evidence of things not seen (see Heb. 11:1). Our faith is made up of substance and evidence. In other words, faith for the believer is not just a natural attitude; it is a spiritual reality. As born-again believers, our faith should be alive and vibrant. In fact, we no longer operate by our own faith as Christians, but we operate by the faith of Christ Himself. It is through faith that we overcome the power of fear. Just like fear is a spirit, faith is a spirit as well. Just as a person who is possessed with the spirit of fear speaks, thinks, and behaves irrationally, those who are possessed with the spirit of faith speak with boldness, think with clarity, and believe with strong conviction that the Word of God is true despite natural evidence to the contrary. We cannot be in faith and fear at the same time; these two are mutually exclusive. When we come to God, we must believe that He is exactly who He says He is and that He will reward us for diligently seeking Him. Faith believes everything God says is the truth; therefore, when God says we have been made righteous, my faith accepts this as my only reality. This is the key to walking in true victory. We must believe the evidence that faith presents more than the evidence fear presents.

PRAYER OF ACTIVATION

Lord God, You are the eternal Giver of good gifts. Show me how good You really are! As You take pleasure in revealing Yourself to me, I delight in knowing You more and more.

I yield to You humbly, so that You may reveal to me the things the devil has sought to hide. Thank you Lord! Amen.

FOR DISCUSSION

1. What does fear attack, and how does it operate?

2. How do we fight back against fear?

3. How have we held to a mistaken vision of who God is? What is He really like, and what does He want most of all?

———— CHAPTER 12 ————

THE POSITION
OF POWER

For the kingdom of God is not in word, but in power.
—1 CORINTHIANS 4:20

I was once a world-class athlete; at least, that's what I told myself. Growing up in a very athletic family, it was very important to be involved in sports. One of my favorite sports was basketball. I would literally play basketball from sunup to sundown. As I developed my basketball skills, I learned something called the triple threat position. It was called the triple threat position because it encompassed dribbling the ball, shooting the ball, and passing the ball—hence the term "triple threat."

I am sure you are wondering what this has to do with the presence of God. Just as there is a triple threat position in sports, there is a triple threat position in your spiritual life. The enemy of your soul is terrified of you getting into this position. What is the position, you may ask? Passionate pursuit, persistent prayer, and powerful praise. I call these the Three Ps of Power.

1. Passionate Pursuit

The Bible tells us in Hebrews 11, *"He that cometh to God must believe that he is, and that he is a rewarder of them that diligently seek him"* (Heb. 11:6). This is what I call passionate pursuit. In other words, God has called us to seek Him with all of our hearts. How do we seek Him? We seek the Lord by delighting in His Word.

Scripture tells us, *"In the beginning was the Word, and the Word was with God, and the Word was God. ...All things were made by Him; and without him was not any thing made that was made"* (John 1:1,3). The word for "beginning" is where we derive the word *archaeology* or the study of foundations (Strong's G746). The Word of God is the foundation of a supernatural life, and it must be the foundation of our passionate pursuit of His presence.

2. Persistent Prayer

The Bible tells us to pray without ceasing. The position of prayer is a position of power. I have heard it said that the most powerful position in the world is on our knees. Prayer prepares us and pushes us into His presence—that is, if you are praying according to God's Word.

3. Powerful Praise

Contrary to popular belief, praise is not optional. It is a necessary response to God's goodness. He not only demands our praise, but His presence commands our praise. Most believers are ignorant of the fact that praise is one of the greatest weapons in the spiritual realm.

In the Book of Joshua, God instructed the Israelites to lift up a shout unto the Lord, and as they obeyed in faith the walls of Jericho came crashing down. The Hebrew word for "praise" is *yadah,* and it literally means "to throw, to cast down, or to give thanks" (Strong's H3034). Contrary to popular belief, praise is not a genre of music characterized by upbeat songs; it is a lifestyle of thanksgiving and appreciation in response to God's hand. God longs to reveal Himself to us. The more you and I engage God in passionate pursuit, persistent prayer, and powerful praise, the more He will manifest Himself to us. God longs to reveal Himself to us. Passionate pursuit leads to persistent power.

NOT MERE WORDS, BUT POWER

It would be an understatement to say that the Church today as a whole doesn't look like the Church in the Book of Acts. Have you ever wondered why? Why don't most believers see the miracles, signs, and wonders that we are promised in Scripture? The Bible assures us that *"these signs shall follow them that believe"* (Mark 16:17). One of the problems that we see in modern church culture is an emphasis on doctrine and philosophy.

The Bible says, *"The kingdom of God is not in word, but in power"* (1 Cor. 4:20). *Word* here is referring to *doctrine.* In other words, doctrine alone will not produce the power. This doesn't mean that doctrine isn't important, but if our doctrine is scripturally sound it must be accompanied by the manifestation of God's supernatural power. Yet there has been a whole generation that has known hermeneutics and homiletics with no demonstration of God's kingdom. We must be people who not only preach the gospel but who experience the power of the gospel.

KEEPERS OF THE SACRED FLAME

The Bible says in Luke 12:35, *"Let your loins be girded about, and your lights burning."* Jesus told the disciples (and He is saying the same to us today) to keep the light burning. We are the candlesticks of the Lord; He has set us forth to illuminate the world around us with His presence and His truth. We have been given the responsibility by God to keep the fire burning. We are responsible for ensuring that our light continues to shine.

When I was a child, my father would take me fishing behind the dam. Because it was very cold, he would light a propane lamp. This lamp served two purposes—to bring light and to bring heat. Once you ignited the lamp, you had to steward the flame to ensure that it continued to burn. The same is true spiritually. God desires for His light to shine in the midst of the darkness. This light permeates the atmosphere around it, creating the spiritual temperature conducive to revival and awakening.

We have been called to be stewards of the sacred flame, just like the ten virgins Jesus spoke about in the Book of Matthew. Five were wise enough to bring along extra oil for their lamps. The other five virgins missed their hour of visitation because they were not prepared. I believe the greatest move of the Spirit of God is coming. In fact, I believe it is already here. The evidence is all around us. Can you feel the atmosphere changing? There is a shift in the spiritual climate. So how do we position ourselves for the move of God?

THE POSITION OF SUBMISSION

The Bible says in First Peter 5:6, *"Humble yourselves therefore under the mighty hand of God, that he may exalt you in due time."* We must submit to God in humility and spiritual hunger. I love that the writer of this epistle used the word *kairos* for "due time." It literally means "opportune time or a divine moment in time" (Strong's G2540). In other words, if we position ourselves in humility we will be at the forefront of God's visitation in the earth.

Revival is instigated by spiritual hunger and humility. Are you desperate enough to see God move in your life? As I travel the world, I realize that people in other countries are desperate to see the power of God manifest in their lives. They are not coddled in the creature comforts that we so regularly indulge in the western world. What do you do when there is not a hospital for a thousand miles? You believe God for a miracle! I believe that there is a stirring taking place in the body of Christ. I believe that people are seeking God like never before and that this pursuit is igniting a flame.

The word *submission* is not often what we think it is. When the Bible speaks of submission, it is simply instructing us to come under the mission. What's the mission?

Matthew 28:19-20 tells us, *"Go ye therefore, and teach all nations, baptizing them in the name of the Father, and of the Son, and of the Holy Ghost: teaching them to observe all things whatsoever I have commanded you: and, lo, I am with you always, even unto the end of the world. Amen."* Jesus commanded us to "teach all nations." What are we commanded to teach them? To do what He taught us! We are called to teach and disciple nations to operate in the culture of the kingdom of God.

We often believe that evangelism means leading someone in a prayer; this is very important, but it is not the complete picture. Jesus wants disciples. In other words, He wants to reproduce Himself in us. You and I have been tasked with coming under the auspices of this mission. We are to honor the great commission—this is what real submission is all about. We must come to a place where His mission becomes our mission.

DEVELOPING SPIRITUAL HUNGER

Jesus said, *"Blessed are they which do hunger and thirst after righteousness: for they shall be filled"* (Matt. 5:6). This is one of the "Beatitudes." In other words, this is an attitude that heaven requires. We are promised that if we hunger and thirst after righteousness, we will be filled. The word *hunger* here is very interesting; it comes from the Greek word *peinaō*, which means "to crave ardently or to seek with earnest desire" (Strong's G3983).

Those who hunger (crave) and thirst for the things of God will have those desires fulfilled. The opposite of spiritual hunger is spiritual apathy. Those who are spiritually apathetic will remain empty. Contrary to popular opinion, spiritual hunger can and must be developed. It is not automatic. Like any craving, the more you feed it the more it will grow. Your hunger determines your desire, your desire determines your desperation, and your desperation determines your manifestation.

I remember when my wife was pregnant with my oldest daughter. She had this overwhelming craving for chicken sandwiches—but not just any chicken sandwich. There was a particular restaurant that she went to every day. I must have consumed more chicken during that period than in any other time in my life.

> In the kingdom of God, the more you eat the hungrier you become.

Usually, when a pregnant woman craves a particular food, it is because her body knows exactly what she needs at that moment for the development of the child. Most doctors tell women not to dismiss their cravings. Spiritually, our cravings symbolize a necessary component to the development of what God has placed on the inside of us. In other words, your hunger is an indication of what you are impregnated with.

If you are feeling a pull by the Holy Spirit to study the Word more, feed the craving. If you are desiring to spend more time in prayer, feed the craving. The more you feed your spiritual cravings, the stronger they will become and the more you will see spiritual growth and manifestation in your life.

REPOSITION YOURSELF

We mentioned earlier the importance of positioning as it relates to us walking in the supernatural. Oftentimes, people ask me, "Why am I not seeing the power of God in my life?" We sometimes ask this question under the assumption that God needs to do something. We subconsciously believe that God needs to change His position, but the truth is that we are the ones who must reposition ourselves in order to experience God's power.

Do you remember the story of the woman with the issue of blood? There is a very important component to that story that we often ignore—she moved into a position to encounter Jesus. She said, *"If I may but touch his garment, I shall be whole"* (Matt. 9:21). She pressed through the crowd in order to get close enough to touch the tallit of our Lord. This required courage and discipline. She did not stay where she was! This was risky, because the law required that any woman with an issue of blood must be put outside the camp; yet she changed her position, both mentally and physically.

If we are going to release the power of God's presence, we must reposition ourselves. Dimensions in the natural are relative to positioning. In other words, we experience things to varying degrees based upon where we are standing. If you are standing behind the stage when a speaker is presenting to an audience, you will see things that the audience will not be able to see. People look smaller from the top of the Eiffel Tower than they do from a 12-foot structure. What you see is dependent upon where you are standing.

If you want different results in your spiritual life, engage God in a different way. When you wake up in the morning, say, "Good morning, Holy Spirit!" Ask God what He desires to reveal to you today. Spend time worshiping Him and delighting in His Word. Change the way you think about the things of God.

RETURN TO YOUR FIRST LOVE

The Bible tells us in Revelation 2:4-5, *"Nevertheless I have somewhat against thee, because thou hast left thy first love. Remember therefore from whence thou art fallen, and repent, and do the first works; or else I will come unto thee quickly, and will remove thy candlestick out of his place, except thou repent."* Jesus admonishes the church in Ephesus to return to her first love. What does this mean?

Do you remember when you first fell in love with someone (or something)? You gave it all of your time and affection. You couldn't wait to see that person or to hear their voice. Do you remember when you first became a believer? Everything was so fresh and exciting. Reading the Bible was an adventure, not a burden. Going to church was a blessing and not a chore. Then, over time, things became stale and dry.

Maybe you have become discouraged by church as usual. What do you do? Repent! What do we mean when we say repent? The word *repent* is our translation for the Greek word *metanoeō,* meaning "to change your mind" (Strong's G3340). It is to turn from that which is dead to that which is alive. Another definition of repentance is "to return to the top." We must go back to that initial place of zeal and passion. We must do what we did in the very beginning of our relationship with God.

> Maintain your intimacy with God. Continue in your love for each other. Keep your relationship with God fresh.

TESTIMONY

One of the many things that I have learned from Dr. Kynan Bridges's teaching ministry is who I truly am as a believer in Jesus Christ, a child of God. Dr. Kynan teaches that as children of God, we have unlimited access to God the Father and we can go to Him about anything and everything. He teaches us that we are accountable for our mindset and that we must choose to agree with what God says about us. I am making that personal in my self-talk every day—I have unlimited access to God, even more so than the access I have to my natural father. I like to compare it to my dad (my earthly dad) in the sense that he is so giving. My dad is and has always been one of the most generous people I have ever known. I can think of many times when he would be on his last bite of something extremely delicious that he was truly enjoying. If one of his children would ask him for some, not even realizing it was all he had left, he freely handed it over and thought nothing of it. He'd wipe his mouth and leave the table smiling. And I know it's because he loves us and desires to hold nothing that he owns back from us. I love this teaching ministry so much because even though I don't always tell myself the truth of who I am right away, I know the truth and can quickly replace the lies when they surface. I realize that God is infinitely more generous and loving than my natural father. And I keep that at the forefront of my mind—that God is my Father, I know His character, I know that He loves me more than I can imagine, and that He will not hold back any good thing from His children.

INTIMACY WITH THE FATHER

One of the most profound statements that Jesus made in the New Testament is found in John 10:30. Jesus said, *"I and my Father are one."* No statement was more provocative. Nothing was more inflammatory to the religious leaders than this very statement. Why? The Pharisees and Sadducees could not wrap their minds around the notion that a man would refer to God as His Father and put Himself in such an intimate standing with a holy God. They, like many people today, believed that God was some distant figure to be revered but never approached. How dare Jesus make such a claim? I have news for you—this statement wasn't just about Him; it was also about the Church.

And now I am no more in the world, but these are in the world, and I come to thee. Holy Father, keep through thine own name those whom thou hast given me, that they may be one, as we are (John 17:11).

> J esus not only declares His oneness with the Father, but through His sacrifice He invited every born-again believer into oneness and intimacy with the Father.

We are one with the Father! This oneness means intimacy and fellowship with Him through Christ Jesus. God is calling us to be consciously intimate with Him. Maybe you feel distant from God. Maybe you don't feel His presence the way you once did. Nevertheless, God is calling you to commune with Him. Jesus said in Revelation 3:20, *"Behold, I stand at the door, and knock: if any man hear my voice, and open the door, I will come in to him, and will sup with him, and he with me."* He is knocking at your door; He is calling you to communion.

PRAYER OF ACTIVATION

Lord God, I open the door to You! I am desperate to see You move in my life; reveal Yourself to me. I will pursue You passionately, praying persistently, and praising You in power. I seek to remain intimate with You so that I can carry Your light and ignite revival. Lord, what do You desire to reveal to me today?

FOR DISCUSSION

1. The enemy of your soul is terrified of you getting into what triple threat position in your spiritual life?

2. What accompanies scripturally sound doctrine?

3. We often believe that evangelism means leading someone in a prayer; this is very important, but it is not the complete picture. Jesus wants disciples. What does that mean?

PRACTICUM

1. God has called us to not only speak about the supernatural but experience it practically. Write down a list of areas in your life that have been stagnant or unproductive and pray intentionally about seeing change in these areas.

2. If you want to know God's intent, meditate in His Word. Meditation determines manifestation. Begin to write down the scriptures that speak to the areas in your life that need to change. Speak these scriptures out daily until you begin to see change.

3. Process the Word by praying. Spend time processing the Word you hear. As you meditate on the Word, it will manifest in your life! Ask God to reignite the cold areas of your heart. Declare that you are returning to your first love. Step out in faith and begin to make yourself available for God to use you in

practical ways (i.e. praying for the sick or ministering to coworkers).

CHAPTER 13

WHEN ETERNITY INVADES TIME

And this is the promise that he hath promised us,
even eternal life.
—1 JOHN 2:25

What if I told you that one of the greatest enemies of the New Testament believer is time? Before you start scratching your head, let me explain. Your ability to walk in the supernatural is contingent upon your ability to recognize and embrace the *now*. Earlier, we talked about the power of now. In other words, we revealed that God lives in the eternal realm, which is outside of the confines of time.

God is not bound by time like we finite beings are. He doesn't view time on the same plane of reality as we do. For example, do you remember the man at the pool of Bethesda? When Jesus encountered this man, he had been physically incapacitated for 38 years. When Jesus asked him the question, "Will you be made whole?" he responded with a time-based answer: "I have been here for 38 years!" In other words, he was bound by the concept of time. He relegated everything God was able to do with the length of time he had been in need of a breakthrough.

Many of you are in that same place right now. You are saying, "I have been in my situation for so many years and yet I have still not seen a breakthrough!" Or maybe you are frustrated that after being a Christian for a long period of time you have not been able to experience the supernatural the way you desire. Either way, your problem is time! What do I mean?

TIME VERSUS TIME

The Bible makes mention of two different types of time. The first is what the Greeks called *chronos*; it's where we get the term *chronological* from. This refers to the natural progression in time as measured in minutes, hours, days, weeks, months, and years. This is what most of us identify with because everything that we do is based on chronos. The other type of time mentioned in Scripture is *kairos*, which deals with an opportune time or the right time. It is literally a divine moment in God's calendar when eternity invades time.

Biblically speaking, kairos is always greater than chronos. In fact, when it comes to the supernatural, kairos always has the last say. This is why Jesus said to the man at the pool of Bethesda, *"Rise, take up thy bed, and walk"* (John 5:8). The word *walk* there is the Greek word *peripateō*, which means "to make due use of opportunity" (Strong's G4043). In other words, Jesus told the man to take advantage of his kairos moment where eternity invaded time and made his impossibility possible.

> Miracles are always *now*. When a miracle manifests, the laws of delay are suspended. Healing can be a process, but miracles are immediate manifestations.

This man did not realize that he was trapped in time, but Jesus stepped into time and liberated him from bondage. Everything about the supernatural lifestyle that Christ wants you to live revolves around your ability to live in the kairos of God. Every moment of every day, God is seeking an invitation to invade your timeline with His eternal realities. The more you learn to live from this vantage point, the more you will live in the power of God on a daily basis.

LIVING IN EXPECTANCY

What are you expecting from God? We have an international prayer call that we conduct Monday through Saturday on behalf of our church. Almost every time I lead the prayer call, I remind the people, "Something good is going to happen to you today!" I intentionally make this statement to create an atmosphere of expectancy. I have heard it said that the atmosphere of expectancy is the breeding ground for miracles. God wants you and me to live in constant and consistent expectancy every single day of our lives. If you fail to believe that, then you won't look for anything from Him. You may know what you want and possibly know some of the things you need from Him, but you still won't look for it if you do not have an attitude of expectancy.

> When you enter God's presence, do you do it with expectation in your heart? This will determine what you receive from God.

Earlier we mentioned that God is able to do exceedingly and abundantly above all we ask or think according to the power that works in us. This power is the presence of God, but it is produced by expectancy. What is expectancy? It's the state of thinking or hoping something will happen, especially something pleasant. It is derived from the Latin word *exspectare*, which means "to look out for." I was surprised to find that many of the English-language synonyms for the word *expectancy* are words we hear or use on a regular basis but rarely associate with having the same meaning as expectation. Some such words are *assumption, belief, confidence, prediction, trust, looking forward to,* and *waiting.* So my question to you is—what are you assuming, believing, putting your confidence in, predicting, trusting, looking forward to, and waiting for?

Living or walking in the Spirit involves anticipation, expectation, seeking, and pressing in for God's presence. Living in continuous expectancy is the key to experiencing the supernatural on a consistent basis.

You ought to anticipate something good happening in your life as a result of your encounter with His presence. David said that we should, *"Enter into his gates with thanksgiving, and into his courts with praise: be thankful unto him, and bless his name"* (Ps. 100:4). We are admonished by the Word of God to enter His gates with thanksgiving. What does this mean? The word translated "gate" literally means "court, tabernacle, or heavenly palace" (Strong's H8179). How can we enter His gates while we are here on earth? We enter His gates by entering into His presence. We give thanks for what God has done in our lives and anticipate Him to move supernaturally on our behalf.

There was a time in my life when I didn't live in expectancy. Sure, I attended worship services and prayed regularly, but I never expected anything radical to take place. What if I told you that God desires for you to have a miraculous encounter every time you pray, worship, or study the Word of God? Ironically, God never approaches us empty-handed. The Bible says:

> *To appoint unto them that mourn in Zion, to give unto them beauty for ashes, the oil of joy for mourning, the garment of praise for the spirit of heaviness; that they might be called trees of righteousness, the planting of the Lord, that he might be glorified* (Isaiah 61:3).

The presence of God is more than a manifestation of God's character and personality; it is a marketplace of His indispensable resources. When we deliberately engage the presence of God, we are engaging with heavenly wealth and abundance. What do I mean? Every time we come into God's presence, there is always a divine transaction that takes place. He gives us beauty for our ashes, the oil of joy in exchange for mourning, and the garment of praise for the spirit of heaviness. There is a spirit called heaviness, which is why many born-again believers are being afflicted by oppression. God wants to take your weakness in exchange for His strength. Hebrews 11:6 reminds us of this truth: *"But without faith it is impossible to please him: for he that cometh to God must believe that he is, and that he is a rewarder of them that diligently seek him."* We know that the biblical, and therefore correct, definition of faith is *"the substance of things hoped for, the evidence of things not seen"* (Heb.

11:1). Active manifestation requires active faith. You must *believe* in order to experience. The catalyst is expectancy! *Decide* to be expectant no matter what.

> Live in expectancy and anticipation of God's promises.

THE MIRACULOUS LIFE

One of the themes of this book and the ethos of this message is the concept of a miraculous life. What if it were possible to live in the miraculous every single day of your life? What does it mean to live a miraculous life? The first thing we must do is define *miraculous*. When we use the term *miraculous* we are referring to something occurring through divine or supernatural intervention or manifesting such power.

A simple way of looking at a miracle is a divine event initiated by God that interrupts or suspends the laws of nature or natural processes. This is what we mean by eternity invading time. An example would be the two fish and five loaves of bread multiplying as recorded in Mark 6, Lazarus being raised from the dead, or the man at the pool of Bethesda being raised up from a bed of affliction. In all these examples, God overrode the laws of nature.

I was once asked, "If it happens every day, how can it still be a miracle?" Most of the significant characters in the Bible experienced miracles consistently; why should we be any different? The God of miracles has not changed and will not change. The key to living in miracles is cultivating an attitude of expectancy along with developing a passionate pursuit of God's presence. The presence of God is the atmosphere where miracles take place. I have seen all types of miracles! This is why I am quite amazed when I hear people say that the gifts of the Spirit and the miracles of the Bible are no more. I wonder which Bible they are reading and what Christianity they are practicing. Miracles are alive and well. Just because many people don't see miracles doesn't mean they are not taking place.

Earlier, we mentioned that there is a difference between living for the presence and living from the presence. There is nothing wrong with being excited about a move of God and anticipating His movement; in fact, I would encourage this. But God's highest agenda is not just to move *for* us; rather, He desires to move in and through us. I have said before that whatever He can get through us, He can get to us. Imagine what it would be like to live your life as a conduit of God's glorious presence. To take this a step further, I want you to imagine that you are partnering with heaven on a daily basis.

GAZING INTO ETERNITY

Several years ago, I was given a very powerful prayer by God. While I was in church one day, I heard a preacher pray, "Father, let me look into Your heart and see the needs of Your people." At the time, I had no idea what the implications of such a prayer would be, but it resonated deeply within me.

One day, I was delivering a message to my church, and before I got into the message, I prayed this prayer, "Father, let me gaze into eternity and see the needs of Your people." All of a sudden, the revelation hit me. God sees us from a miraculous perspective. Earlier, I talked about seeing from heaven's perspective. This is so important to the life of the believer that it bears repeating. Every miracle that Jesus performed, He saw in the heart of the Father. He affirms this in His own Word where He tells them, *"I say unto you, The Son can do nothing of himself, but what he seeth the Father do: for what things soever he doeth, these also doeth the Son likewise"* (John 5:19). If we are continuously being formed into the image of Christ, this means we should continuously become more and more like Him. As He is, so are we. As God's eternal Son, He came to show us how to live as God's eternal children, His eternal people. How can we see into the heart of God? We come to learn the Father's heart through prayer, spending deliberate, quality time with God. You won't know the Father's heart if the extent of your prayer life is, "Lord, thank You for this food, bless it," or through rote bedtime prayers. To see from heaven's perspective, the eternal prospective, you must tap into God's heart through a life of true communion and fellowship with Him.

As I stated before, God is not limited to time. He lives outside of time. As His offspring, you and I have been given the power to live outside of time as well. No, you are not limited by your current circumstances, because your current circumstances have nothing to do with your destiny in God. What do you think about eternity? Is where you are now where you see yourself in eternity? If your answer is no, then you have already completed a key step—seeing yourself beyond where you currently are. The power of God is more capable than the nature of your situation. Needless to say, the power of God is farther beyond your situation than you are even able to imagine. We cannot begin to fathom the depths of His strength and power. Ask yourself, "Is this my eternal destiny? Is this the end result of my life in Christ?" Nope! Keep in mind that you are already living in eternity because eternal life with God began the moment you accepted Christ as your Savior and Lord of your life. Even when Jesus was here on the earth in a human body, He transcended time. He always focused on where He was going, no matter what was going on around Him. The Scriptures repeatedly tell us that He kept His face set toward Jerusalem; we know that He made many stops along the way, had many conversations, changed numerous lives, and constantly healed hordes of people. Yet, even in the midst of the ministering and miracles and persecution from the religious leaders, the Lord remained focused on His assignment. In a human body, He maintained His eternal perspective, which included the cross for sin, the grave for our old lives, and His return to heaven to be with His Father and give us the new life.

When Christ prayed, He knew without a doubt that His Father heard Him and that He would give Him what He asked, because He knew that God had it to give and would do so willingly. He even told God in front of the people, *"I knew that thou hearest me always: but because of the people which stand by I said it, that they may believe that thou hast sent me"* (John 11:42). *This* is the confidence we are supposed to have in God's power. First, that the Almighty God, our heavenly Father, hears us when we pray and that He will do what we ask of Him.

THE PRIESTHOOD OF THE BELIEVER

Earlier, we talked a great deal about the authority of the believer. We know that it is extremely important for believers to understand their identity in Christ and take authority over the enemy, but it is equally important for us to understand the priesthood that we have been called to serve. The Bible says that we are kings and priests. What does this mean? Many believers in modern times have placed a strong emphasis on spiritual warfare, but there has been less of an emphasis on consecration and holiness.

One day the Lord spoke to me and said, "You need to consecrate yourself." I thought to myself, "I don't have a bunch of sin in my life!" But this was not what God was addressing. Consecration deals with believers setting themselves apart from the things that would hinder us from entering into His presence in the fullness God intends. We must separate from anything that is unclean, distracting, or compromising so that we can develop a greater sensitivity to the manifest presence of God.

It is time for the Church to graduate from struggling with sin as a way of life and move on to perfection—abiding in the will of God. Everyone falls short at times, but if we are truly pursuing His presence, our highest agenda is not to overcome sin but to please the lover of our soul. This can be quite tricky! Most of my Christian experience was based upon making sure I didn't do anything that upset God and trying to avoid His wrath, but God revealed to me that there was a higher calling.

What if we would simply love God for who He is? What if people would bask in His presence, not because they want something or because they are "in trouble" but because they are completely overwhelmed by His goodness? Paul wrote in the Book of Philippians, *"That I may know him, and the power of his resurrection"* (Phil. 3:10).

PROTOCOLS OF THE PRESENCE

How do we enter God's presence, and what does it look like? I believe that if we would simply learn God's way of doing things, we would experience greater success in the realm of supernatural living. Previously, we discussed the pattern of worship found in the Old Testament as revealed by Jacob's ladder. We know that we are to ascend and descend. But I believe there is so much more. David wrote in the Psalms:

> *Know ye that the Lord he is God: it is he that hath made us, and not we ourselves; we are his people, and the sheep of his pasture. Enter into his gates with thanksgiving, and into his courts with praise: be thankful unto him, and bless*

his name. For the Lord is good; his mercy is everlasting; and his truth endureth to all generations (Psalm 100:3-5).

PRAYER OF ACTIVATION

Lord, I come into Your presence with expectation in my heart. I want to live every moment in expectancy and anticipation of Your promises. Here in Your presence, I live in the kairos moment, the eternal now where Your miracles are manifest. Lord, I invite You into my timeline—bring Your eternal realities! I receive them today! Amen.

FOR DISCUSSION

1. What is chronos time? What is kairos time?

2. What is expectancy and why is it important?

3. What is the role of a king? What is the role of a priest? What do these roles look like in your life, as a believer who is a king and priest according to Scripture?

CHAPTER 14

LIFE MORE ABUNDANTLY

The thief cometh not, but for to steal, and to kill,
and to destroy: I am come that they might have life,
and that they might have it more abundantly.

—JOHN 10:10

Jesus promised us an abundant life. What was the abundant life that Jesus referred to? The word used here is *zoe*, which means life full and overflowing (Strong's G2222). To delve deeper, it is the life that God possesses within Himself; it is eternal life, plain and simple. Contrary to popular opinion (as we have discussed before), eternal life is *not* in the future; it is now! Right now, those of us who have placed our faith and trust in Christ have eternal life. This is a Spirit-filled life.

And be not drunk with wine, wherein is excess; but be filled with the Spirit (Ephesians 5:18).

The Word of God tells us that God has called His Church to be filled with His Spirit. This is a very simple truth that many in the body of Christ have not yet embraced and/or have yet to experience. As a matter of fact, the Bible commands us to be filled with the Spirit. We see this in Ephesians 5:18, where it clearly says, "be filled."

The Holy Spirit is one of the most important persons in our lives. Some would even say that He is the most important person in our lives because He is the one who reveals Jesus Christ and glorifies the Father. When we speak of the Holy Spirit, who are we really speaking of? Some cults and false religions teach that He is a force of some sort, but we know based on Scripture that He is not a force; He is a person. However, this person does possess power, and He releases that power in our lives as we yield to Him.

THE PERSON OF THE HOLY SPIRIT

I want to spend a few moments highlighting the importance of the person of the Holy Spirit. Number one—He is the third person of the Trinity, and He was in the beginning of creation. Number two—He is the Spirit who anointed Jesus and gave Him the supernatural power to carry out His earthly ministry. Number three—He is the Spirit who raised Jesus from the dead. Number four—He is the regenerative agent in salvation who quickens our dead human spirit, makes us alive in Christ, and joins us to the Lord as one Spirit. These are some serious attributes!

The question remains—what does it mean to be filled with the Spirit, and what does the Spirit-filled life look like? I am glad you asked! To be filled has a few meanings that we will explore here. In Ephesians 5:18, the phrase *be filled* is derived from the Greek word *pleroo,* and this means to make full, to supply liberally, to fill to the brim (Strong's G4137). It is important to note that this is a verb that is expressed in the imperative tone. In other words, it is a command from God. God commands us to be filled to the brim with the Holy Ghost!

Once we become born again, being filled with the Spirit in this way is not optional. The implication in this passage is that of continuity and control. This type of infilling is not a one-time event; this is a continual filling. This is not just about a religious experience but a yielding of control. God wants you and me as believers to be dominated by the Holy Spirit.

I believe that every Christian should yield to the Holy Spirit more and more every single day. By doing this, we are being filled in the sense that His power and nature are filling us to the brim. We are no longer carnal but spiritual. We are no longer lustful but loving. We are no longer judgmental but merciful. Why? Because the more we are filled with the Holy Ghost, the more the Holy Spirit's influence saturates every area of our life. This is so important that it cannot be understated. The only life for the Christian is the Spirit-filled life.

HOLY SPIRIT BAPTISM

In Acts 2, we see another type of infilling. I believe that this Holy Spirit baptism is the impetus for the infilling that we are commanded to experience in Ephesians 5. In the Book of Acts, the Bible says:

> *And when the day of Pentecost was fully come, they were all with one accord in one place. And suddenly there came*

a sound from heaven as of a rushing mighty wind, and it filled all the house where they were sitting. And there appeared unto them cloven tongues like as of fire, and it sat upon each of them. And they were all filled with the Holy Ghost, and began to speak with other tongues, as the Spirit gave them utterance (Acts 2:1-4).

This was a historical event for the New Testament Church. In fact, this event was so momentous that Jesus told the disciples to wait for it. It was so important to Jesus that He instructed His disciples to not go anywhere until they experienced this promise. That's right! Jesus promised this.

In Acts 1:4, the Word says, *"And, being assembled together with them, commanded them that they should not depart from Jerusalem, but wait for the promise of the Father, which, saith he, ye have heard of me."* He did not refer to this supernatural manifestation as *a* promise, but He referred to this experience as *the* promise. This was the big one! This was the promise that Jesus had spoken of for the past three and a half years of His earthly ministry. What was the promise specifically?

In Acts 1:8, we see exactly what this promise is: *"But ye shall receive power, after that the Holy Ghost is come upon you: and ye shall be witnesses unto me both in Jerusalem, and in all Judaea, and in Samaria, and unto the uttermost part of the earth."* This was the baptism in the Holy Ghost. Jesus said that once the disciples received the baptism of the Holy Ghost, they would receive power to become witnesses. This power was like nothing they had ever seen or experienced prior to His ascension.

POWER FOR LIVING

Once again, the word for "power" that Jesus used is the Greek word *dunamis,* which means power residing in a thing by virtue of its nature

(Strong's G1411). Dunamis is where we get the English word *dynamite*; in other words, this is explosive power. Now, in Luke 10:19 Jesus said, *"Behold, I give unto you power to tread on serpents and scorpions, and over all the power of the enemy: and nothing shall by any means hurt you."* This statement was made prior to His ascension. The question is—if Jesus had already given them power before He left, why did they need more? Well, the word for "power" in Luke 10:19 is the word *exousia*, which means authority (Strong's G1849).

Whether we realize it or not, we need power to live the abundant life. We need power to operate in the earth on a daily basis. Jesus made this very clear. The disciples already had authority by virtue of their relationship with Jesus. This authority was delegated to them by Jesus; what they needed to be witnesses was power. What is the difference?

Authority is always for external use. For example, the only real purpose of a police officer's badge is so that people who are not police officers can recognize their authority. If a law enforcement officer pulled you over, you would not yield to them until you saw their badge, which represents their authority. However, a police officer does not use their badge with their spouse and children. It is only for external use.

The disciples needed authority in order to exercise kingdom government over demon spirits. Every believer in Jesus has the right and authority to cast out demons; we have the name of Jesus for that purpose. However, power (*dunamis*) is a completely different issue altogether.

Power, as it is defined in Acts 1:8, is internal in nature. It is the divine ability to execute or manifest something. Power is the ability to exercise authority. It is primarily internal in its usage. For example, an officer has the ability to act even when he or she is off duty. They can carry their gun with them to their place of residence, and it has the same effect as it would have if they were on duty. They have the nature of a police officer. The instincts, the ability to react, and the desire to protect stay with the officer 24 hours a day. It is on the inside of them. This is the type of power Jesus was referring to in the Book of Acts. This power can only come through the baptism of the Holy Ghost.

What do I mean by the term *baptism*? This is the Greek word *baptize,* which means to immerse or submerge (Strong's G907). Jesus said that when He left, His disciples would be submerged in the fire of the Holy Ghost. This is what took place in Acts. They were all filled (*pimplemi,* Strong's G4130) with the Holy Ghost with the initial evidence of speaking in other tongues as the Spirit gave them utterance. Some people argue about tongues, but I believe that it is a divine language that is alive and well today, and it is absolutely necessary for the Church to walk in the supernatural power of God.

The disciples received a supernatural empowerment that enabled them to proclaim the message of the kingdom of God with boldness, purity, and conviction. As a matter of fact, by the end of the apostle Peter's sermon in Acts 2, the people were so supernaturally convicted that 3,000 souls were added to the Church in one day. Now that's an altar! What was the secret weapon? The baptism in the Holy Ghost! Every believer must experience this Holy Spirit baptism if they want to live a life of victory.

SO MUCH MORE!

There is so much more to living a Spirit-empowered life than meets the eye. Fortunately for me, I was raised in a Spirit-filled church and I saw the power of God from an early age, yet I knew in my heart that there was more. We have used semantics and vain philosophies to suppress the power of God for far too long. No wonder there are so many churches today experiencing powerlessness and defeat. Whole denominations have rejected the most important person on the earth—the

Holy Spirit. Yet He is the most precious gift given to the Church. Every born-again believer has the blood-bought right to be Spirit filled and to speak in other tongues as the Holy Spirit enables them.

In Acts 2:6-8 we can see that while the disciples began to speak in other tongues, it released supernatural power into the atmosphere. This power drew the nations together. People heard in their own native tongue the wonderful works of God. What an amazing demonstration of God's power!

Did you know that one of the purposes of the outpouring of the Holy Ghost is to unify the Church? He (the Holy Spirit) is the only person who can unite people regardless of race, gender, nationality, or ethnicity. He is the only one who can transcend all language barriers and cause the body of Christ to hear one heavenly sound. We need the Holy Spirit! Oh, if only the church would return to her New Testament roots.

If the baptism of the Holy Spirit was necessary for the early Church, then it is just as necessary for us today. We need the baptism of the Holy Spirit! It is important to note that the purpose of the baptism of the Holy Spirit is not to just speak in tongues. The gift of tongues is a sign. The Bible says in First Corinthians 14:21-22:

> *In the law it is written, With men of other tongues and other lips will I speak unto this people; and yet for all that will they not hear me, saith the Lord. Wherefore tongues are for a sign, not to them that believe, but to them that believe not: but prophesying serveth not for them that believe not, but for them which believe.*

PRAYING IN THE SPIRIT

As I mentioned before, I believe that Scripture is clear about the importance of tongues. We must pray in tongues for the edification of our spirit man. We must pray in tongues in order to speak forth mysteries in the spirit realm, but ultimately it is a symbol of the fulfillment of a promise. God promised in the book of Joel that He would pour out His Spirit on all flesh. The day of Pentecost marked the manifestation of that promise to the early Church. However, speaking in tongues is not the main evidence or main purpose of being filled with the Holy Spirit; it is an initial evidence.

The main purpose of the infilling of the Holy Spirit is to be a witness. The word witness is derived from the Greek word *martys*, which literally means to testify in a legal sense (Strong's G3144). It is one who bears witness of the truth of something. It is where we get the English word *martyr* from.

The idea is that the early Church was to bear witness to the resurrection of Jesus Christ by dying to themselves and testifying of the kingdom of God. How did they perform this task? By living a resurrected life! How were they able to live a resurrected life? By being filled with the Holy Ghost. Praying in the Spirit is one of the ways we release the supernatural power of God. Every time we pray in tongues we are activating the spiritual dynamo on the inside of us.

THE MYSTERY OF THE SPIRIT

The manifestation of this supernatural power is demonstrated in every area of our lives. When we are filled with the same Spirit who raised Jesus from the dead, our lives are full of victory. We are no longer seeking our own wills or agendas, but we have been crucified with

Christ. This is, in fact, the complete evidence of being filled with the Holy Ghost. Throughout the years, I have seen people around me who spoke with tongues but whose lives were full of defeat.

How can you speak with tongues and claim that you are filled with the Holy Spirit when your heart is still full of hate, bitterness, and rebellion against God? How can we say that we are full of the Holy Ghost when our lives are not characterized by holiness? It has to do with a wrong understanding of what it really means to live Spirit-filled lives.

It is not enough to speak in tongues. We must have an overflow of supernatural anointing that enables us to live the way Jesus lived when He walked the earth nearly 2000 years ago. It means that we have the power to live above sin and to deny our fleshly desires. It means that we can say "no" to adultery, fornication, and pornography. It means that we have the sovereign ability to forgive those who have wounded us and to love the unlovable. This is the evidence that we have been immersed in the Spirit of the living God.

Make no mistake, I speak in tongues fluently and frequently. I believe that it is one of the most necessary and powerful weapons that any believer can have in their arsenal. This arsenal is to be coupled with a lifestyle that glorifies God. We have no reason to be defeated when the third person of the Trinity is resident in our spirit.

We have heavenly power available to us at all times. Why should we be any less powerful than the early Church? As a matter of fact, I believe that we should be more powerful! The early Church did not have the completed Bible to read and know exactly what to do. We have been given the explosive combination of the Spirit and the Word. This mixture releases supernatural power for every believer.

Can you imagine how the Church would look if we settled the issue of sin and moved on to perfection? Can you imagine the impact the body of Christ will have on the world when we are full of the love of God? Speaking in tongues is just the beginning of the Spirit-filled life!

HOW TO OPERATE IN THE ANOINTING

The heavenly realm is available to me here and now, but it is important for me to learn how to operate in the anointing of God to see the power of God demonstrated. Christ is the head of every believer. His anointing flows down to us (the body). Just like the oil flows down Aaron's beard, we are the recipients of the anointing that flows from Christ, the Anointed One.

What is the anointing? Simply put, the anointing is the yoke-destroying, burden-removing power of God, dynamic in its working. Jesus needed the anointing to carry out His earthly ministry, and you and I need the anointing to live supernaturally. In the next chapter, we will talk about the difference between the anointing and the glory, but for now I want to take a moment and highlight the importance of God's precious anointing. You must understand the anointing in order to operate in the anointing. Your level of understanding affects your level of recognition.

> An anointing you fail to recognize is an anointing you fail to release.

One definition that I heard for the anointing is "the supernatural equipment to get the job done." The anointing is meant to get results. Jesus got results! The Bible says in Acts 10:38, *"How God anointed*

Jesus of Nazareth with the Holy Ghost and with power, who went about doing good, and healing all that were oppressed of the devil; for God was with him." Notice that Jesus was anointed to *do good*. The anointing is always for action, never inaction. Even though Jesus was in the earth, He operated in the realm of the supernatural. The anointing causes you to operate in another realm (see Isa. 10:27). It is important for you to understand that you have already been anointed according to First John 2:27. Even though we have been anointed already, we need faith to unlock it. Faith recognizes and releases the anointing. By faith, we *release the anointing* God has placed within us by the Holy Spirit.

You will find the greatest manifestation of the anointing when you do what you have been called and designed to do.

> Learn to recognize the anointing in you. As you steward the anointing, it gets stronger.

PRAYER OF ACTIVATION

Lord, help me to recognize the anointing You have placed within me. I commit to steward the calling You have placed upon my life, with the empowering aid of the Holy Spirit. As I pray in tongues, teach me how to operate in the anointing. Holy Spirit, I welcome You into my life, for You empower me to manifest the kingdom. Amen.

FOR DISCUSSION

1. What does it mean to be filled with the Spirit, and what does the Spirit-filled life look like?

2. What is the difference between power and authority?

3. What is the main purpose of the infilling of the Holy Spirit?

CHAPTER 15

THE GLORY OF GOD

For God, who commanded the light to shine
out of darkness, hath shined in our hearts,
to give the light of the knowledge of the
glory of God in the face of Jesus Christ.
—2 CORINTHIANS 4:6

M ore than ever, God is desiring to manifest His glory in and through our lives. He wants to manifest Himself in ways you have never experienced before. This is why the enemy has waged an all-out war against the body of Christ—because he does not want the Church to see the glory of God revealed in this generation. However, the Bible promises that the glory of the latter house will be greater than the former. What is the glory of God? In Psalm 19:1, the Bible says, *"The heavens declare the glory of God; and the firmament sheweth his handywork."* The word *glory* comes from the Hebrew word *kabowd*, which means honor, abundance, or weight (Strong's H3519). The early rabbis described it as the shekinah glory or the manifest presence of God. It was so heavy that the priests were said to literally fall to their knees when the glory was revealed.

Another way to describe the glory of God is the atmosphere of heaven. Moses prayed, *"Show me Your glory!"* (See Exodus 33:18.) The word *glory* includes the connotation of reputation or splendor. God's glory is an expression of His character, esteem, and reputation. The glory of God is one of the most misunderstood things in the modern Church. Spiritually speaking, you cannot separate God's glory from His honor. Until the Church truly learns to honor God's presence, we will never see His glory. Many Christians erroneously mistake a feeling of bliss with the glory of God. You have probably heard people say, "I felt the glory of God in that place!" The truth is, the glory is not simply felt; it is seen. This is why Moses asked God to show him His glory. Moses was already acquainted with God's voice and His presence, but he had never witnessed His glory. To witness the glory of God in raw form was a death sentence under the Old Testament.

Scripture tells us that God is the light that no man can touch or approach. It is difficult to fathom the awesome splendor of God's manifest presence. This is why the Bible says that the angels cry "holy, holy, holy" night and day before His presence. The glory of God creates an internal atmosphere of revelation. This means that for the rest of eternity, we will be in a continual state of awe and wonder as God unveils Himself, forever. Think about this: if God did something as unremarkable as slightly moving one of His fingers or a toe, another aspect of His glory would be revealed! Do you realize how awesome God is? Moses had no idea what he was really asking. Because of man's sinful nature, he had no legal right to stand in the presence of God. This is why God sent His Son, Jesus Christ, to create for us a new way of living.

THE GLORY WITHIN

The Bible tells us that God who commanded the light to shine out of darkness has commanded the light of His glory, in the face of Jesus Christ, to shine in our hearts. Simply put, God through Jesus has placed the glory within us. If only the Church understood the glory of God! The glory of God is an atmosphere of infinite possibility. It is literally heaven on earth. Earlier, we talked about days of heaven on earth, and God's desire to tabernacle with man. This is not a far-reaching concept or religious philosophy. This is something that has very practical implications. This is why God gave us His precious Holy Spirit, so that we would not only have the anointing, but we would be able to live in the glory. After I had my first heavenly visitation years ago, God begin to deal with me about the glory. He showed me that many churches have never experienced the glory of God, because many believers have never experienced the glory of God. Before the fall of humanity, Adam and Eve were clothed in the glory of God; this is why they were naked and unashamed. Eden comes from a Hebrew word which literally means "spot." In other words, Eden represented a spot of the manifestation of God's glory. It was literally heaven on earth. When man fell, he was thrust out of that atmosphere into a natural existence, where he would toil for the rest of his days. I want you to see the contrast here: before the glory, there was instant manifestation. After the glory left, there was hard work and toiling; this is the difference between the glorious Christian life and the defeated Christian life. Jesus said that He came to seek and to save that which was lost. Man lost the glory of God as a result of sin. Jesus came to restore God's glory to man, made possible as a result of His sacrificial death on the cross.

MADE FOR HIS PRESENCE

Earlier, we stated that mankind was made in the image of God. Not only were we made in the image of God, but we were made for the glory of God. We are handcrafted by God to glorify Him and to dwell in His presence. We know that ultimately we shall receive glorified bodies that will enable us to live in heaven throughout eternity, but from a spiritual perspective you and I can interact with the presence of God here and now. Why? Because God already lives on the inside of you. What makes you think that the Holy Spirit lives inside of you but the glory of God dwells elsewhere? I have heard respectable theologians argue that as human beings we cannot encounter the manifest presence of God or we will die. This was true before the cross, but not now. In Acts 2, the glory came down in the house where the disciples were gathered; instead of people falling dead, 3,000 people were born again. Moses was in the glory for 40 days and 40 nights, and when he came out of it his face shone like the sun—that same glory killed the rebellious Israelites in the Old Testament. It's the nature of the person who interacts with the glory that determines the outcome. Fire can consume or refine depending on the nature of the object that it touches. Before Christ, the presence of God was a terror to us because we didn't have the Holy Spirit living on the inside; however, now that we are born again, the glory of God is an atmosphere into which He invites every believer.

THE DIVINE EXCHANGE

I want you to imagine that two individuals are performing the waltz. This dance is based upon an exchange where each partner is facilitating the other and engaging the other. The onlookers are so enthralled by its beauty that they are unaware of the intricacies involved in orchestrating this dance; this is what the glory of God is like. I said earlier that the word *glory* involves honor. In other words, the Father is honoring the Son and the Son is pouring His love on the Father, while the Holy Spirit is facilitating the exchange. The combination of this divine exchange creates the atmosphere that we call the glory of God. In this atmosphere, miracles are commonplace. If we want to see revival in our churches, if we want to see miracles, signs, and wonders, the key is creating an atmosphere conducive for the glory of God to manifest.

Every time we welcome the presence of God, we are inviting the Father, Son, and Holy Spirit to engage in this divine dance; once we step into it, we are caught up in an ecstasy and a splendor that we cannot begin to imagine. It is like being in the front-row seat of a world-renowned orchestra performance and experiencing with intimate detail every chord and melody. I believe that God desires to redefine what worship really is. He wants to invite us to an experience with His presence that will alter the very fabric of the Church as we know it. We will not be able to limit worship to a 45-minute portion of the service or even a concert, but it will become an infectious culture of honoring God the Father, acknowledging the Son, and welcoming the Holy Spirit.

No Honor, No Glory

It is important to understand that what you honor determines what you attract. In this generation of instant gratification, we often fall into the trap of desiring rewards without investment. It is kind of like a marriage where two individuals want intimacy, yet they have not invested time and care into the relationship. If we want sustained revival, we must invest time and intentionality into cultivating God's presence in our lives. The time is coming, and now is, when creative miracles are commonplace. I have personally witnessed the explosive power of the glory of God. In fact, most times I allow God's glory to do all of the work. On one occasion, I was in a meeting where all we did was worship. While we were worshiping, there was a Muslim man in the room. This man was physically healed of an injury that he had for many years. At the end of the meeting, he came forward and confessed his faith in Christ Jesus. Make no mistake, the preaching of the word of God is absolutely necessary, but it is time for the Church to experience an outpouring of the glory of God where His Word is received. Might I remind you that before God spoke in Genesis 1, His presence was already moving in the atmosphere? There is a direct correlation between the movement of God's Spirit and the declaration of God's Word; one cannot take place without the other.

CONTINUAL OUTPOURING OF HIS GLORY

There is a hot spring where my parents grew up in southern Georgia. This spring is very popular, and many people attribute medicinal properties to the water that flows out of it. People come from all over the world to collect water from this spring. It has been flowing since the time my parents were children, and it is still flowing now. This spring reminds me of the presence of God. There is a continual outpouring of God's presence and power that is available to this generation. Jesus said, *"He that believeth on me, as the scripture hath said, out of his belly shall flow rivers of living water"* (John 7:38). That flow refers to a continual outpouring. Everything that you need in order to experience the supernatural is in the presence of God. I remember the first time the glory of God entered my room. I was speechless! There were no words to describe the feelings that I felt and the splendor that I witnessed. The Lord granted me a taste of heaven on earth.

THE ANOINTING VERSUS THE GLORY

It is important to distinguish between the anointing and the glory. There is a very distinct difference between the two. The anointing is God's divine enablement for a particular service. It comes from the Greek word *charisma* or *chrió*, which means "to smear, unguent, or ointment" (Strong's G5545). It was used for medicinal purposes in ancient times to treat certain conditions. It was also used to consecrate the priests for service in the temple. Simply put, the anointing is God's supernatural power to accomplish a specific assignment. The word *glory*, on the other hand, comes from the Greek word *doxa*, which means "magnificence or majesty" (Strong's G1391). It is analogous to the splendor of a king and his kingdom. The anointing is when God empowers someone to do something; the glory is when He does it Himself. When God manifests Himself, the anointing becomes obsolete, no longer necessary for that moment. The anointing is power or work in the earth, but the glory is His presence manifested from heaven.

> The glory of God brings revelation, but anointing is the power to walk in the revelation—whatever has been revealed.

I teach that there are three dimensions to the supernatural. The first is faith, the second is the anointing, and the third is the glory. This is analogous to the three dimensions of the Old Testament tabernacles—the outer court, the inner court, and the Holy of Holies.

THE PATTERN OF THE TABERNACLE

There are two tabernacles described in the Old Testament—the tabernacle of Moses constructed in the wilderness and the tabernacle of David. The tabernacle of Moses was a type of Christ and the tabernacle of David was a type of the New Testament believer (i.e. the Church). The tabernacles of the Old Testament, specifically the tabernacle of David, revealed a divine pattern of prayer, intercession, and intimacy with the Holy Spirit in the lives of New Testament believers. I want to show you that the outer court of the tabernacle of David was a type of the believer preparing themselves to serve the Lord daily in praise and meditation on the Word of God, the inner court represents the place of intercession and communion with God, and the Holy of Holies is a type and shadow of the Holy Spirit indwelling and manifesting in the life of the born-again believer.

1.

THE PLACE OF PRAISE AND MEDITATION

In the Old Testament tabernacle of Moses, there was an outer court, inner court, and the Holy of Holies. Both the tabernacle of Moses and the tabernacle of David shared the outer court and Holy Place. The outer court was a place where every one of the Israelites could congregate and bring their sacrifices to the priest. The Bible records, *"And thou shalt make the court of the tabernacle: for the south side southward there shall be hangings for the court of fine twined linen of an hundred cubits long for one side"* (Exod. 27:9). The outer court was also a place of preparation. The Israelites would prepare their offering to the Lord in the outer court of the tabernacle. Once the offering was prepared, it would be given to the priest to place on the brazen altar. This is a type and shadow for the New Testament believer. David said, *"Enter into his gates with thanksgiving, and into his courts with praise: be thankful unto him, and bless his name. For the Lord is good; his mercy is everlasting; and his truth endureth to all generations"* (Ps. 100:4-5). The word *praise* here is the Hebrew word *tĕhillah* meaning praise, adoration, and thanksgiving (Strong's H8416). The outer court was not only a place of preparation but also a place of praise. As the Israelites praised and adored God for His goodness, they were prepared to sacrifice to Him.

As New Testament believers, every day of our lives should be filled with thanksgiving and praise. As we "tabernacle" through our day, we are to give thanks to God and prepare our hearts to serve Him. The Bible says, *"Be careful for nothing; but in every thing by prayer and supplication with thanksgiving let your requests be made known unto God"* (Phil. 4:6). The writer of Hebrews admonishes the Church, *"By him therefore let us offer the sacrifice of praise to God continually, that is, the fruit of our lips giving thanks to his name"* (Heb. 13:15). Notice that the writer refers to thanksgiving as a "sacrifice." Just as the Israelites congregated in the outer court to offer praise and sacrifice on the brazen altar, so must the born-again believer offer the sacrifice of praise in thanksgiving for Christ's sacrifice on the fiery altar of redemption.

The outer court was not just a place of praise; it was also a place of cleansing. In the outer court was the brass laver (see Exod. 30:18). The purpose of the brass laver was the ceremonial washing (cleansing) of the priest. Before the priest could offer sacrifices, he first needed to undergo the washing of his hands and feet. In the New Testament we are referred to as royal priests (see 1 Pet. 2:9). The brass laver represents the Word of God. Through the Word of God our minds and hearts are cleansed daily. Jesus said, *"Now ye are clean through the word which I have spoken unto you"* (John 15:3). Paul wrote in Ephesians 5, *"That he might sanctify and cleanse it with the washing of water by the word"* (Eph. 5:26).

As we meditate in the Word of God, we are cleansed in our mind and conscience and thus prepared to serve the Lord with our whole hearts. Jesus washed His disciples' feet before going to the cross. By doing so, He was preparing the disciples to "walk out" their service to God in the earth. The laver was also made of brass, which meant that it was able to act as a mirror for the priest. As the priest washed his hands and feet in the brass laver, he could also see his own reflection and further examine himself. This was a type and shadow of the Word of God acting as our spiritual mirror for perfect self-examination. The apostle James wrote:

> *Wherefore lay apart all filthiness and superfluity of naughtiness, and receive with meekness the engrafted word, which is able to save your souls. But be ye doers of the word, and not hearers only, deceiving your own selves. For if any be a hearer of the word, and not a doer, he is like unto a man beholding his natural face in a glass: for he beholdeth himself, and goeth his way, and straightway forgetteth what manner of man he was. But whoso looketh into the perfect law of liberty, and continueth therein, he being not a forgetful hearer, but a doer of the work, this man shall be blessed in his deed* (James 1:21-25).

As you can see, the Word of God is the means of cleansing our mind and examining our heart.

2.
THE PLACE OF INTERCESSION AND COMMUNION

The next portion of the tabernacle was the inner court or Holy Place. This area of the tabernacle was not accessible to the congregants of the outer court. Only the Aaronic priests were permitted into the Holy Place. There was an altar of incense in which God commanded the incense to be burned perpetually. The Bible records, *"And thou shalt make an altar to burn incense upon: of shittim wood shalt thou make it"* (Exod. 30:1). The inner court (especially the altar of incense) was a type and shadow of New Covenant intercession. The word *intercession* comes from the Greek word *hyperentygchanō*, which means "to intercede for one or to come in the behalf of another" (Strong's G5241). Simply put, to intercede implies to "stand in the gap" for another person in prayer.

The incense represents the prayers of the saints. Revelation says, *"And the smoke of the incense, which came with the prayers of the saints, ascended up before God out of the angel's hand"* (Rev. 8:4). The incense was to be burned perpetually, symbolizing the continuity of the prayer life of the born-again believer. The Bible says, *"Pray without ceasing"* (1 Thess. 5:17). New Testament believers are called to a life of intercession. The Bible says, *"Likewise the Spirit also helpeth our infirmities: for we know not what we should pray for as we ought: but the Spirit itself maketh intercession for us with groanings which cannot be uttered"* (Rom. 8:26). The Holy Spirit empowers the New Testament believer to *"pray without ceasing"* by offering up continual intercession through and for the believer.

The inner court was also a place of communion with God. Within the inner court (Holy Place) was the table of showbread. This term, *showbread*, is rendered in the Hebrew "bread of the presence" or "bread of faces." In other words, the showbread was a type and shadow of the believer's perpetual communion with God before His face. Bread always represents communion in the Bible. Jesus taught His disciples to pray saying, *"Give us this day our daily bread"* (Matt. 6:11). We are to commune with the Lord daily. Jesus modeled this paradigm by waking up early in the morning to seek the face of God. Aaron was commanded by God to place fresh bread on the table every morning.

3.
THE INDWELLING HOLY SPIRIT

Beyond the inner court was the Holy of Holies (or "holiest of all"). In the tabernacle of Moses, the Holy of Holies was veiled by a seven-foot curtain separating those in the inner court from the Ark of the Covenant. In the tabernacle of David, there was no veil. I do not believe this was an oversight on the part of King David but a prophetic type of the New Testament believer. This distinction in the two tabernacles is very important. Under the Law, the priests were not permitted beyond the veil. Only the high priest could enter the Holy of Holies once a year to offer sacrifices on behalf of the people. The high priest would pour the blood of sacrifice on the Mercy Seat. This was referred to as the Day of Atonement or Yom Kippur. The purpose of Yom Kippur was to atone or cover the sins of the nation of Israel for the past year. No one except the high priest was allowed to gaze upon the Ark of the Covenant, let alone enter, in the pattern that Moses was given.

One unauthorized touch could mean the end of a person's life. Yet in the tabernacle of David there was no veil. Why? Hebrews 10 explains this perfectly:

> *Having therefore, brethren, boldness to enter into the holiest by the blood of Jesus, by a new and living way, which he hath consecrated for us, through the veil, that is to say, his flesh; and having an high priest over the house of God; let us draw near with a true heart in full assurance of faith, having our hearts sprinkled from an evil conscience, and our bodies washed with pure water* (Hebrews 10:19-22).

Jesus, as our great High Priest, went into the Holiest of All and sprinkled His blood upon the Mercy Seat, granting us eternal access into the Holiest of All. In addition to granting us access "through the veil," we have now become the tabernacle. The Holy of Holies was an Old Testament shadow of the New Testament believer's body as the dwelling place of the Holy Spirit. Paul the apostle declares, *"What? know ye not that your body is the temple of the Holy Ghost which is in you, which ye have of God, and ye are not your own?"* (1 Cor. 6:19). The word *temple* comes from the Greek word *naos*, which literally means "sacred edifice or Holy of Holies" (Strong's G3485). Our body has become the ark that houses the manifest presence of God. In other words, Jesus not only gave us access to the Holy of Holies, but He gave the Holy of Holies access into us.

CONCLUSION

Isn't God good? Even back in the Old Testament, He gave us the tabernacle of David as a prophetic type and shadow of the spiritual life of the New Testament believer. He showed us through the outer court that there would be a place of preparation through praise and the cleansing of the Word of God. He also gave us the inner court or Holy Place as a prophetic picture of intercession and communion with God—the believer's continual fellowship and communion before the face of God. Most precious of all, He shows us through the Holy of Holies how the Holy Spirit would one day come to dwell within the New Testament believer.

When we really get a hold of these deep biblical truths, our lives will never be the same. This wonderful God has been planning to live within each of us since the beginning of time; what a miracle! What an honor! The God who created the universe designed you for Himself.

When you begin to carry His presence wherever you go, you will know the true depth of your purpose and your calling in Him. Let us all open our hearts wide and welcome His presence!

PRAYER OF ACTIVATION

Father, we thank You today. Holy Spirit, we ask that You take control of the atmosphere and, Lord, speak in ways that man cannot communicate. Holy Spirit, we ask that You touch the very core and reservoir of our being. Lord, this is not a message to the mind but it's a message to the spirit and soul. Lord, we trust You now to do that which only You can do. Give me the tongue of the learned to speak a word in season. Awaken my ears to hear as the learned and to receive what the Spirit is saying to the church. Let every word that I speak be that which is ordained and commissioned by You, that You alone may be glorified, in Jesus' name.

I'm ready to receive. I'm ready to walk in my assignment. I'm ready to move forward. In the mighty name of Jesus, I decree this now. And, Lord, seal it in my spirit where the enemy won't be able to touch it or me, in the mighty name of Jesus. Amen and amen!

FOR DISCUSSION

1. What is the difference between the anointing and the glory?

2. How does the Old Testament provide a picture foreshadowing the life of the New Testament believer?

3. What should our focus be if we wish to steward the glory of God's presence?

ABOUT THE AUTHOR

At the tender age of 15, Pastor Kynan committed his life to Jesus Christ and was subsequently filled with the Holy Spirit. After getting involved in his local church, God made His call manifest to Kynan audibly. For many years, he served in the local church and was involved with various ministries. But after running from the call of God, he was finally arrested by the Holy Spirit. Several years ago the Lord told Kynan to begin a teaching ministry in Tampa, Florida, where the vision for Grace and Peace Global Fellowship was birthed.

Paul wrote, *"For if by one man's offense death reigned by one; much more they which receive abundance of grace and of the gift of righteousness shall reign in life by one, Jesus Christ"* (Romans 5:17). This is the vision and mission of Grace and Peace Global Fellowship ministry: to see the person, power, and presence of Jesus Christ manifested in the lives of people everywhere so they will reign in life. Through this ministry, they desire to see millions of souls saved and restored through the gospel of Jesus Christ. The ministry will accomplish this mission by proclaiming the unadulterated, life-changing Word of God. The outreach ministry serves as the catalyst to spread this message. Every week they provide resources to people so they might become more conscious of Christ's love for them and enter into the fullness of His finished work, thereby being positioned to walk in their God-ordained assignment, namely the great commission, as outlined in Matthew 28:19-20.

The ministry's weekly podcast (FaithTalk) serves as a platform to discuss various issues in the body of Christ and around the world, shedding light on those issues through the illumination of God's Word. Grace and Peace Global Fellowship is committed to spreading the gospel through their preaching ministry, speaking engagements, teaching resources, and Internet and media platforms.

To date they have reached countless numbers of people with the gospel. Through the combined efforts of their weekly outreach ministry and new media resources, they have exposed thousands to the gospel of grace every single week. Currently they are communicating God's Word to people in North America, India, Haiti, and Nigeria. The ministry is engaging in several outreach efforts, which have a global impact as well.

Pastor Kynan is committed to allowing the power and anointing of the Holy Spirit to flow through him and touch God's people. He is a committed husband to Gloria, father to five beautiful children, Ella, Naomi, Isaac, Israel, and Anna Grace, and a mentor to many ministry partners and friends. For information on booking, prayer requests, or supporting this ministry, write to:

Kynan Bridges Ministries
P.O. Box 159
Ruskin, FL 33575
1.800.516.7038
Or visit us at:
www.kynanbridges.com